StarCars

BEKI
ADAM

OSPREY

Page 1 The Spy Who Soaked Me—Agent 007
James Bond gets away from it all by escaping to
the Med in his Lotus Esprit

Previous page These two cars, a '38 Willys coupé
and a '56 Ford F100 pickup, were used in a TV ad

Right Since the Keystone Kops the police have
borne the brunt of car-chase action as this shot
from *Gone In 60 Seconds* shows

Published in 1987 by Osprey Publishing Limited
27A Floral Street, London WC2E 9DP
Member company of the George Philip Group

British Library Cataloguing in Publication Data
Adam, Beki
   Star cars.
   1. Automobiles—Customizing
   I. Title
   629.2'222   TL145
ISBN 0-85045-803-X

Editor Tony Thacker
Design 20/20 Graphics

Filmset by Tameside Filmsetting Limited,
Ashton-under-Lyne, Lancashire
Printed in Hong Kong

Contents

Ever since the Keystone Kops rattled across our flickering screens in their Model Ts, there has been an affinity between the audience and the automobile. The car was saying something about the characters, and the cinema-goers could recognize what it was saying. The Model Ts were also skidding, skittering and sliding, and all the time they did that, the audience paid attention. The eye cannot be averted when the brain says something exciting is going to happen, and if you're making a film, the more it does that, the better—and so we had the basic foundations of the stunt.

If a car is equipped with a plethora of gadgets, it's an indication that the driver is just as multi-talented, and usually of the super-hero mould. If the car is chromed, finned and very definitely fifties, then the driver is still at high school and usually having a ball. If the car is sporty, fast and European, then the driver is good looking (supposedly), rich and successful. If the car is basically a wreck, but runs on a meaty V8, and is American, then the driver is a no-frills, determined, ruthless type, and he's probably after somebody.

Thus, without even realizing it, we have categorized almost every car that appears in a movie, and therefore, we have categorized its driver. It didn't take the movie moguls long to catch on to the fact that the car could say just as much about their characters as the actor himself. The day they did, the car became an inherent part of the movies. Action, as they say, speaks louder than words.

Photo courtesy of the Estate of Elvis Presley

This pink Cadillac Fleetwood was Elvis' most famous car. It was his mother's favourite and one of his most treasured possessions— photographed outside the famous Heartbreak Hotel, although it now takes pride of place at the Graceland display

The principle applied to the silver screen, that a car says as much about a person as anything can, is also true of life away from the camera.

The world of showbusiness is full of varied and colourful personalities; it is almost a pre-set requirement of being a star. It follows that to look at a celebrity, and the car he, or she, drives, is a privileged insight into the person behind the public image. This, along with the usual criticism that a stunning car is just a blatant display of wealth, has put many famous faces off sharing their passion with the rest of us. Sadly, as time goes on, this seems to happen more and more, but there was a time gone past, when the media pressure wasn't so great, and all anybody wanted to do was get behind that wheel and drive. Even more sad, is that some of the auto enthusiasts of that era are no longer alive. Elvis had his Cadillacs, Keith Moon had his wild and whacky T-bucket, John Bonham had his beautiful hot rods, Liberace had anything that sparkled, James Dean had his Porsche, and Steve McQueen had his love of racing. This book is a tribute to those enthusiasts who are no longer with us, but whose memory will never fade.

American wax—a young Elvis polishes one of his Cadillacs for a fanzine photo session, circa 1956. Sadly, the car is thought to have been destroyed

Photo courtesy of the Estate of Elvis Presley

James Dean

He was on his way to Salinas to take his newly-acquired Porsche racing; he had been looking forward to it for weeks. It was 30 September 1955, and Warner Brothers biggest star was on holiday, having only finished filming *Giant* with Elizabeth Taylor and Rock Hudson the day before. He only got as far as the intersection of Highway 41 and Highway 46, near Cholame, California—he was killed instantly when his Porsche Spyder was hit on its left front wing by a Ford. The impact, Dean was travelling at around 85 mph, totally destroyed the left-hand side of his car, but his mechanic Rolf Weutherich escaped from the passenger seat almost unscathed, as did Donald Turnipseed, the driver of the Ford. Nobody really knows how it happened, and no one was ever held responsible, it was irrelevant, James Dean was dead.

He was only 24, but what he achieved, and what he left behind him, will never be repeated. James Dean is a legend, remembered for simply playing himself.

He had made three films: *East Of Eden*, *Rebel Without A Cause* and *Giant*. His performances were superb, though the quality of them often, and rather sadly, seems to be lost within the legend. Admittedly, his untimely death has a great deal to do with his status in today's society as a teenage cult hero; he cannot age, so the image cannot die, but it should be remembered that almost every actor, however great, has at least one performance to be ashamed of—James Dean had none.

His passion for fast cars and bikes was not, as some may think, a passing whim. He had a burning desire to drive fast; he had owned other cars, and driven them the same way. He was young, he was successful, and he was good looking; but he lived life differently to other people, he cut it fine.

Terence Steven McQueen managed, undeniably, to cram much more than the average lifetime into the 50 years that he was given. Born on 24 March 1930, his first years were by no means easy, his wayward youth leading him to reform school. Fortunately, his talent finally led him to drama school, and it was at drama school that he first caught the racing bug—he had bought a Harley-Davidson and used to run it at Long Island City drag events.

McQueen had to wait until he was 26 before he made his movie début as a 'two-line extra' in *Somebody Up There Likes Me* which, incidentally, starred another young hopeful, Paul Newman. By the time screen recognition came in 1960 with *The Magnificent Seven*, McQueen was hurtling around the auto circuits in his newly-purchased 1600 Porsche. The real

fun started in 1963, with the release of *The Great Escape*. McQueen was now wielding enough box-office power to influence his films, and if that meant including the odd car or bike chase, then so be it. The closing scenes of *The Great Escape*, which saw McQueen stunt-riding a modified Triumph, were the epitome of his life.

The year 1965 saw the release of *The Cincinatti Kid*, followed a year later by *The Sand Pebbles*, for which he received his only Oscar nomination. With the arrival of 1968 came both *The Thomas Crown Affair*, co-starring Faye Dunaway, and *Bullitt*, co-starring the Mustang.

The Thomas Crown Affair featured some skilful off-roading in a Myers Manx dune buggy, powered by a 180 hp Corvair engine. It told the story of a millionaire who, just for kicks, robs

Steve McQueen

McQueen's big love in life was motorcycles; when he died, in 1980, his collection numbered more than 100. These were sold at an auction of his effects along with a '57 Jaguar XK-SS, a couple of old Packards, a Chrysler, a Hudson and an army Jeep. There were no signs of the Porsche 917 or Speedster he was reputed to own

Photo: Rex Features Ltd

a bank. It also told of McQueen's latest 'just for kicks' passion off-camera. Having been forbidden to race sports cars by his studio—a decision prompted by a crash he'd had while messing around on the Brands Hatch track in England—he had turned his attention to off-roading, a sport that was fast gaining popularity in the late 1960s. While everybody else was in the cinema watching *The Thomas Crown Affair*, McQueen was bouncing about in another dune buggy, the 'Baja Boot', competing in the Stardust 7-Eleven race in Las Vegas. He was also competing in the Mexican 1000 and hurling jeeps through muddy river-beds in the Riverside National Four-Wheel-Drive Grand Prix, as well as around LA's Ascot Speedway.

Then, as if all that activity wasn't enough, came the release of *Bullitt*, which contains what is indisputably the most famous and dramatic car chase on celluloid. The chase was conceived by, and partly driven by (remember the studio restrictions), McQueen himself. It consisted of, if there are any who do not remember, a GT 390 Mustang and a Dodge Charger, with the beauty and roller-coaster hills of San Francisco being used to full advantage. McQueen wins, of course, by forcing the Dodge off the road and into a gas station which, upon impact with the totally out-of-control Charger, explodes in a mass of flames. The stunt, obviously highly dangerous, was carried out by what is called a 'tow and release' technique. The cars appear to be side by side, travelling at immense speed, but the Mustang is actually towing the Dodge, which has a dummy at the wheel. At a given point, the driver of the Mustang pulls a release lever, which disconnects the cars and causes the Charger to head off in the direction of the gas station, and the end of the film.

Mr McQueen managed successfully to sneak back behind the wheel of a sports car in 1970. He co-drove a Porsche 908 in the 12-hour endurance race at Sebring, Florida, and finished just 23.8 seconds behind Mario Andretti—no mean achievement by any standards, and especially commendable on this occasion: McQueen was driving with a special shoe, because a short time before the race he had broken his foot in six places!

McQueen used the streets of San Francisco as the backdrop for his 1968 film *Bullitt*. The car in question was a '68 Ford Mustang GT 390 two-door fastback coupé which produced 325 bhp. It proved ideal for McQueen's cunning stunts which he handled himself. The attacking Dodge was driven by veteran Hollywood stunt driver Bill Hickman, famous for his driving in *The French Connection*

Right Off-roading, in or on anything, was always a favourite pastime of McQueen's. He raced this four-wheel-drive 'Baja Boot' in both the Stardust 7-Eleven race around Las Vegas and the Mexican 1000, a 1000-mile race down the Baja peninsula

And then there was *Le Mans*, a landmark in the silver screen's relationship with the automobile. The story behind it is fascinating. McQueen had nurtured the idea of a film about this, the most exciting of endurance races, for many years. His idea was to actually compete in the real Le Mans, with a camera mounted on the car, and to record his true lap times. Then they were to somehow 'weave this footage into the script'—the story line, as one can imagine, was not at the top of his list of priorities. The preparation for a project of this type was immense; McQueen, as we know, was already practising a year earlier at Sebring. With two victories at Holtsville and Phoenix, the path appeared to be running smoothly until, in his third qualifying race, disaster struck. The gearbox blew, and he was forced, amongst showering metal, to control a gearless car heading into a bend at over 100 mph. It is a

reflection of his driving ability that he succeeded in bringing the car to a halt without injury. This was, however, not enough for his movie company, who refused to allow him to compete in the actual Le Mans race as had been planned. Under McQueen's watchful, although now restricted, eye, the film went ahead. Real Le Mans footage was used, and the track hired for restaged races, with McQueen at the wheel of a 600 hp Porsche 917.

McQueen had fulfilled his dream, and although the script was weak, resulting in poor box-office takings, the exceptionally fine camera work and the dedication to detail made *Le Mans* one of the finest, and most accurate, automotive films ever to reach the screen. Which is all Steve McQueen ever wanted.

In the film he always wanted to make, *Le Mans*, McQueen drove this Porsche 917

McQueen's other film for 1968 was *The Thomas Crown Affair*, which featured him off-roading in this 180 bhp flat-six Chevrolet Corvair-powered Myers Manx buggy

This story, like so many in this book, begins in the early 1960s when Jeff was either cruising Chelsea's King's Road or playing guitar with the Yardbirds. At the time he owned a rare '63 split-window Corvette, but had spotted a '32 Ford sedan street rod in the Portobello Road and decided to swap the Vette for it and £800. It was to be the first of many.

By 1965 he was solo and touring America where he saw his first real rods. He just could not resist buying one, a California-style Model T called The Boston Strangler, and shipping it back to Britain. Open-topped Ts are fine for the summer, but when it rains, as it so often does in England, something with a roof, bonnet and wings is preferable. Jeff therefore decided to fix up the sedan. After a lot of work, a lot of fun and a lot of American magazines, Jeff realized that what he had, as good as it was, wasn't quite right. OK, it was a '32 Ford, but a li'l Deuce coupé it was not.

If you want the right car you go to the right place, and in 1967 Jeff found himself surrounded by 1200 of America's finest at the Street Rod Nationals in Memphis, Tennessee. He drove away with what he had come for—a '32 Ford three-window Deuce coupé. It was an ex-drag racer with a hot 327 cu. in. Chevy but he drove it the 700 miles to Chicago and had it flown home. Now he had a real rod and it was time to move the T on to fellow guitarist John Bonham of Led Zeppelin.

Above She's a '34 all right, and all steel and almost all original except for 350 cu. in. Chevy V8 power, Mustang brakes, Chevy Vega steering, American Racing five-spoke wheels, and that dramatic roof chop which is 4½ in. at the front, tapering to 4 in. at the rear

Right This beautiful black three-window coupé was bought in Yorkshire with restoration in mind, but after a short drive Jeff decided to update it with a new Brizio hot rod chassis and Chevy power

16

Jeff Beck

The silver sedan was bought as just a body which, according to the hieroglyphics on the side, had once been used as a taxi in San Francisco. It too now resides on a Brizio chassis powered by a Chevy

The candy red coupé was purchased 20 years ago and has been rebuilt more than once. At the moment it rides on a Chevy-powered Deuce Factory chassis and five-spoke wheels

One street rod just did not seem to be enough when you liked so many styles, but that wasn't a problem until George Lucas released his film *American Graffiti*. Like so many people who saw the film, Jeff just had to have that canary-yellow coupé. The difference was he did something about it. He called an American magazine and asked the editor to find him another coupé, this time of the five-window variety. Within an hour he had found a car and eventually the deal was done and another Deuce coupé was on its way to England.

By now, Jeff really had the hots for rods and in 1973 bought three more: a roadster, another five-window, and an American Tudor sedan called Super Prune which had been a class winner at the Oakland Roadster Show. He also decided it was time for more T, so he imported all the parts from America and made it himself. Not content, he went back to the Street Rod Nationals in 1978 and bought another Tudor sedan. That brought his total up to seven '32 Fords and a bucket of T.

Enough for anybody you might think and you'd be right—well, almost. The English weather called for constant maintenance and there was ever a need to update and improve the cars. The three-window was getting a new chassis, a roof chop and candy-red paint when Jeff decided he had to have a '34 Ford. Work on the others stopped while a three-window coupé body and a bunch of parts were shipped over from California. That car was completed in record time. As for the others, it was good news and bad. The roadster met with a tree one night and was subsequently shipped back

Above American Graffiti influenced every hot rodder, not least Jeff, who built one of the more faithful replicas using parts imported from America. Sadly, it too is illegal for England with drag slicks

Above right The big orange was Jeff's first fibreglass car. For it he found yet another Chevy V8—with so many cars it pays to have interchangeable parts—and rodded his own original chassis. Unfortunately, with no fenders it's no fun in England

to California to be rebuilt. It's there ready to use whenever he is in America. Super Prune also went home, the English weather having destroyed its show shine. Sadly, the second five-window went as well and has been sold, but Jeff managed to replace it with another, original, three-window found almost on his doorstep in Yorkshire, that too has now been rodded. The second sedan has had its second rebuild. The '34 got a coat of Porsche red paint to replace the original gunmetal grey, and just recently he has built himself another roadster, the first fibreglass car he has built. It is not the first he has owned though; the garage also contains a classic '62 Chevrolet Corvette and, for everyday driving, an '84 model. There was also a '69 convertible Corvette but that was sold to drummer Cozy Powell. Quite a collection from a chance-sighting in a London side street in the 1960s.

20

James Bond

The Living Daylights

It is now estimated that the total number of cinema admissions to the James Bond films stands at well over one and a half billion—that's almost half the world's population. Bond is not just Great Britain's most successful secret agent, he is also hero of the most successful screen series of all time.

Bond is back, to celebrate a quarter of a century at the box office, with *The Living Daylights*, his 15th mission. Timothy Dalton is the new 007, fourth in a line-up that started with Sean Connery, then George Lazenby (*On Her Majesty's Secret Service*), and finally Roger Moore.

Throughout Bond's 25-year career, there have been two things that he always makes sure he is never without. A beautiful woman, and a beautiful car.

The Living Daylights is, of course, no exception. Maryam d'Abo plays the beautiful Kara, who Bond meets on his first assignment, to ensure the safe defection of a Russian general. The car heralds the return of the Aston Martin. This time, however, it's not just one DB5—it's an Aston Martin Volante and the hardtop V8 saloon version. Both cars run on 5.4-litre V8 engines of standard specification. Nevertheless, they are good for 0–60 mph in 7 seconds, with a top speed of 150 mph. Each engine is, by the way, totally the responsibility of a single man at the factory, and when his work is complete, his name is engraved on a brass plaque fitted to the engine. The Vantage and Volante are two models from the six that Aston produce. The others are the V8 Vantage, slightly faster than James' version; the V8 Vantage Volante, which is the fastest convertible in the world; the four-seater Lagonda; and the Vantage Zagato, a limited-edition version with Italian body styling.

In their 70-year history, Aston Martin have produced just over 10,000 cars; when Detroit was in full swing, that's the number they were churning out every 20 minutes.

The DB5s

The Bond series began back in 1962 with Sean Connery starring in *Dr No*. It was followed a year later by *From Russia With Love*, and the year after that saw the release of *Goldfinger*, and the entrance of Bond's most famous car, the Aston Martin DB5.

Bond's mission in *Goldfinger* was to foil the arch-criminal Auric Goldfinger, played by German actor Gert Frobe in his first English-speaking part. Along with that beautiful Aston, James had the help of Pussy Galore, played by Honor Blackman. Auric was a self-confessed gold addict who, unfortunately, did not possess the Midas touch, so simply resorted to evil practices in an attempt to quench his insatiable desire.

Major Boothroyd, known as Q for the first time in *Goldfinger*, comes to the rescue with a hurriedly-equipped DB5, the gadgets including machine guns, an oil dispenser, smoke emitter, bullet-proof shields, an ejector seat, a saw blade rotating on the wheel hubs, and, of course, a homer terminal.

Needless to say, with all that equipment, Bond defeats Goldfinger in the end. But, as 007 has shown us so many times in the past, it is not the end, merely a pause for breath. It is only a year until Bond and his Aston are called out to save the world yet again, in 1965, this time from the evil Emilio Largo. *Thunderball* features James with the same DB5, and ultimately, after fierce underwater scenes, an assassination from a rocket-firing motor bike, and a final one-to-one confrontation, the same result is achieved—he wins.

On Her Majesty's Secret Service, released in 1969, starred George Lazenby and another Aston, this time the DB6. We then saw the Astons disappear from 007's equipment for over 15 years. They have now returned in *The Living Daylights*, but in the meantime, enter the Lotus.

In 1977 *The Spy Who Loved Me*, the tenth episode in the Bond series, came to our screens. It heralded the appearance of a Lotus Esprit in a series of impressive stunts, the most memorable being the underwater sequence.

The stunt started with what turned out to be the most dangerous part of filming. Bond, in the Lotus, is being chased and fired at by a helicopter. To create the impression of bullets just missing the car, small amounts of explosive were planted on steel plates and triggered by remote control. However, when the car was travelling at over 90 mph, one such explosion went wrong and the steel plate was fired up into the bodywork, missing a tyre by centimetres.

When the Lotus finally plunged into the water, and the audience gasped, that familiar theme music echoed through the cinema, and the Esprit miraculously sprouted fins. Perry Submarines in the Bahamas marinized the Lotus body, i.e. turned it into a 'wet submarine', by adding four electric motors, sealed batteries, a ballast tank, and a life support system for the driver. As the Lotus emerged from the salty Atlantic waters, much to the surprise of a few innocent sunbathers, it completed one of the most enjoyable and effective stunts in cinema history.

The next Bond film to feature a Lotus was *For Your Eyes Only*, released two years later in 1981. This time it was a Turbo Esprit fitted with ski mounts and designed and constructed by Lotus.

The first model that appeared in the film was equipped with a revolutionary, ultimate-deterent burglar alarm. Touch it, and both you and the car get blown up. The instructions given to Lotus were to prepare a car for such a shot, but ensure that from 5 ft away it would look, to the nut and bolt, like a real Lotus. What they actually created was a half-upholstered shell, with a space-frame chassis, and specially hinged doors. They also cut into the roof, so that, upon explosion, the car would blow up in the 'required order': the roof, the doors, the bonnet and, finally, the passenger seats flying out through the roof. The stunt, much to everybody's relief, worked first time. The original white Lotus that had been used at the beginning of the film, before it was blown up, was then resprayed in metallic copper, re-upholstered in a new warm gold leather trim, and finally fitted with the ski mounts. This was actually done to two identical cars, it being always wiser to have two, just in case. Lotus also ensure that police dispensation is granted to allow two identical cars to be driven around with the same number plates, for the sake of simplicity.

Lotus are always happy to supply United Artists with their cars, as are Aston Martin, so we can rest assured that Bond and his quintessentially English sports cars will be seducing the silver screen for a good few years to come.

The Lotus cars

James Garner's relationship with cars and the screen can be very closely paralleled with that of McQueen and Newman. Much of Garner's private life has been spent either on, or beside, the track. He also made *Grand Prix*, a film that, like McQueen's *Le Mans* and Newman's *Winning*, captured the excitement and energy generated by the racing circuits of the world.

Garner underwent extensive training by the well-respected Bob Bondurant high-performance driving school in preparation for the filming of *Grand Prix*, although ever since high school he had been hurtling about in various cars. His close involvement and dedication to the film is the major reason for its authenticity. He did a large amount of the actual driving himself, which dispensed with the need for 'process shots'—taken with the vehicle stationary, and a back-projection. It is largely due to this active role that he had to complete the last few months of filming totally uninsured. It might also have had something to do with the fact that the underwriters discovered that he had been driving around Belgium at over 135 mph, in the wet, and that he was also scheduled to drive in the highly dangerous fire sequences to be filmed at Brands Hatch—this was something that they simply could not tolerate. McQueen had also experienced similar problems while filming *Le Mans*.

Grand Prix was released in 1966 and immediately picked up two Oscars for its sound engineers and editing team. They had used a stunning new technique called multi-screen projection, which involves the use of several images on the screen at one time.

The late 1960s and early 1970s saw Garner become increasingly interested in off-road racing, a booming sport at that time. He was a regular competitor in all the major US off-road events, including the Mexican 1000, Baja 500, Mint 400, and the Stardust 7-Eleven. The race names, by the way, roughly indicate the length of the course, except for the 7-Eleven which was named after its sponsors, a chain of grocery stores that opened from 7 am until 11 pm. It may well be that, at one time or another, he drove in the same races as Steve McQueen, who was also competing in these events. In 1969 Garner showed his endurance capabilities by driving all 832 miles of the Mexican 1000 by himself, completing 26 hours of non-stop driving—at the age of 41!

Garner's philosophy was simple: he felt it was much safer to be completely enclosed in an off-roader fitted with a full roll-cage and bouncing about mountain ranges, than it was to be behind the wheel of a Formula One car—and both were better than the freeway!

His interests, however, did encompass formula-type racing, and he was a regular attendant at the United States Auto Club races, such as the Indy 500, although he took a more passive role of either pit area inspector, or he publicized the sport by making celebrity appearances.

It is dedication like this that makes James Garner such a special figure in the world of cars and stars. He is, of course, still out there, doing what he loves best.

The year was 1983, and no one, least of all Billy Gibbons, leader of Texan band ZZ Top, could have realized the impact that his newly completed 1933 Ford coupé was about to have on the world of popular music. ZZ Top had been together, in one form or another, since 1969, and had already experienced considerable success. What they had not done up until that time, though, was inject inspiration and give direction back to the lagging rock music scene; and they certainly hadn't woken up the world. However, Billy's three-window coupé was just about to change all that.

Gibbons, always on the lookout for something new, had spotted Pete and Jake, the talented hot-rodding duo, resting their two beautiful '34 coupés on the way to a show. Billy stopped, got talking, and got addicted. He had to have a rod, and he had to have it how he wanted it— he had to have it built.

The construction, from start to finish, of a hot rod always involves a large number of different people and workshops, each specializing in their own field, but the man who can be credited with most of the work on Eliminator is Don 'Buffy' Thelen, one of California's most respected rodders.

The body, with the exception of the hand-formed aluminium side-opening three-piece hood, is all-original 1933 Ford steel and rare.

Photo courtesy of *Autocar*

Nevertheless, Buffy's first major task was to chop 3 inches out of the roof, without which a rod simply isn't hot. As well as 3 inches of height, Buffy discarded the bumpers, the headlights, which were replaced with some from a '34 model, and the rear lights which went in favour of classic '39 Ford tear-drops.

Pete and Jake engineered that ready-to-pounce look by fitting a 4-inch lower Super Bell axle to the original chassis rails. Power is supplied by a 350 cu. in. Chevy engine, fitted with a four-barrel Holley carb, and personalized valve covers bearing the ZZ Top logo.

The maroon and beige leather and cloth interior was stitched by Vic Kitchens, the dashboard was designed by Reed Lillard, Vintage Air sorted out the ventilation, and artist Kenny Youngblood designed the famous double Zees that were laid over the red acrylic lacquer.

There simply is not enough space to include all the names and details that relate to the '33.

Suffice to say congratulations to all concerned; they can be content in the knowledge that they had created *the* hot rod of the 1980s.

There are actually two Eliminators cruising around, and they are both official; the second one was created while Mark I was touring England, and it became apparent that one could not cope with the demand, so Chuck Lombardo at California Street Rods knocked up another one in record time, although the second model was made from fibreglass.

Photo: © SIPA-PRESS Rex Features Ltd

The two latest additions to the ZZ Top fold are a '59 Volkswagen and a Pontiac Limousine. Spearheaded by Billy Gibbons, a Bug was on the cards the minute Billy drove past, and subsequently called in on, a local VW show. One of the exhibitors at the show was Dale Johns of D & D Speciality Cars in Arkansas. For Dale, Billy's visit became the start of a five-month project to build what he calls a 'totally radical Bug'.

Having set such high standards with the Eliminator, Billy and the boys wanted much more than a standard Convertible Beetle. They have, of course, in their usual style, done it again. Dale was right—it is totally radical.

Based on a 1970 chassis, the '59 bodyshell has had its fair share of modifications from one-piece windows (a rare sight on Convertibles) to the suicide doors, and it would be hard not to notice that the '59 is practically sitting on the road—that was achieved by lowering the front suspension by about 5 inches. The power comes from a 1835 cc engine, fitted with a single Dell'Orto carb, while the fumes find their way out via a modified Monza exhaust. One of the weirdest alterations was the addition of hidden rectangular headlights, which flip open electronically. These boys have thought of everything. The ZZ Top logo, applied after all the work was completed, has become rather like an award, given only if the vehicle lives up to expectations. You will notice that the double Zees are in place; you will also notice that this is one wild and wicked wagon.

Finally, the ZZ Top Limo. Based on a '48 Pontiac, the Limo was originally found in a 'forested region' by James Emerson, who gave it to Billy as he wanted to see it restored. Was that a wise move?

The first thing Billy did was send the car out west, to California Street Rods, owned by Chuck Lombardo. The boys there, never ones to

4 ft, and added a late-model drivetrain and suspension package to bring the ride up to modern standards. Racing Head Services fitted a 454 cu. in. Chevy big-block; it was balanced, blueprinted, blown, and ready to blast. Maximum blast, by the way, is 160 mph. The Limo has independent front and rear suspension, rides on Goodrich Comp T/A tyres and Center Line Champion 500 re in wheels

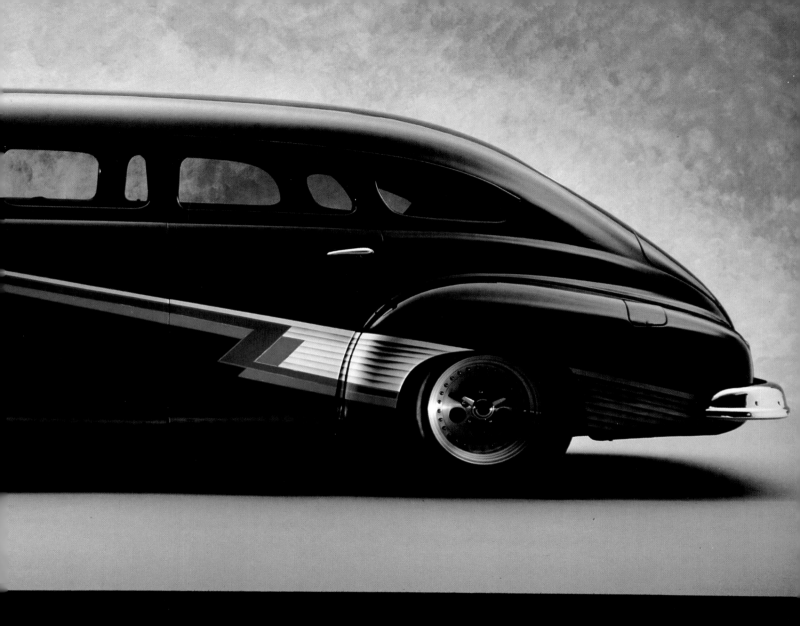

Back in the lounge area there is a 1000-watt stereo rig that was installed by South West Sony in Houston. The lounge area also possesses the usual 'Zzeen' functions—video, bar, and fresh-frozen-margarita machine, all supplied by Fortune Equipment of Memphis.

The black belladonna with the ritual Zee Zee graphics then went for its final touch to the King of Kuts, Dick Dean ('Dean's my name,

chopping's my game'). Dick sliced 4 inches out of the roof in a record eight days—which was just in time for the newly completed ZZ Velcro-mobile to be on set for shooting the final scene of *Velcro Fly*.

In the last four years we've seen the Eliminator, the VW, and the Limo. Whatever next? As they say at the end of their videos: 'To be continued . . . . .'

Photo courtesy of *Autocar*

Jools Holland does not pass unnoticed. Neither does his car. One is an exceptionally talented television presenter, musician and DJ; the other is a 1959 Corvette.

Jools' love of the automobile started, like Steve McQueen's and so many others, with bikes. As a teenager he was absolutely crazy about Velocettes, English bikes of high engineering standards, with their rather agricultural looks being of secondary importance—it was an acquired taste.

Holland's passion, in line with practicality, went from two wheels to four. A series of Rovers and then a Humber Hawk finally led to a 1952 Buick, and his first American car. The Buick with its eight-cylinder overhead-valve engine gave around 124 bhp, not exactly quick. It was replaced by another Buick, this time a '49 Convertible, which went on to play an integral role in helping Jools to obtain his present car, the Corvette.

The object of his desire ever since he had spotted it as a teenager, Jools finally managed to convince the owner (a Buick fan) to take his '49 in part-exchange. Deal struck, and Holland happy, the Corvette sped off to its new home.

Jools Holland

Anyone that has ever driven, or even ridden in, a 1958–62 model Corvette will understand that, unlike Buicks, you simply cannot get bored. So here the chain of Holland motors comes to a halt.

The performance figures provided by the Vette's 283 cu. in. V8 engine made it almost unbeatable in the late 1950s, but would not be considered so impressive by today's standards. However, point this out to any third-generation Corvette owner, adding the indisputable fact that they handle like a nightmare, and he will look at you in disbelief.

When discussing the joys of driving a '59 Vette, as Mr Holland will gladly explain, such facts are irrelevant. The V8 rumble, on the other hand, coupled with the lurching acceleration and that beautifully-chromed curvaceous body, are what it's all about.

Jools does talk of wishing to own other cars, maybe an Aston Martin (preferably the DB6), or perhaps a '58 Buick Century, but one has the sneaking feeling that, like a Velocette Venom he bought when he was 19, this immaculate 1950s classic will not be up for grabs.

Jeff Lynne, lead singer with the rock group ELO, is the proud owner of this wonderful AMG Mercedes.

It is based on the 560 E, an automatic four-door saloon that Mercedes designed to be quick but not electrifying; the standard version reaches 60 mph in over 7 seconds and doesn't go much faster than 120. Unless, that is, you hand it over to AMG, the prestigious West German tuners and body-kit specialists.

The process is simple: you buy the basic car, hand it over to AMG with a cheque for approximately £40,000, and they will give you back a car like Jeff's. At first sight the AMG conversion will appear to be little more than a body-kitted Merc, but, as it disappears down the road, and you realize that the first sighting was the only one you will get, it becomes apparent that an AMG conversion isn't just a pretty face.

Jeff's 190 bhp straight-six engine was hauled out to be replaced by the 5.6-litre V8 that is normally fitted to the 560 SEC, Mercedes' fastest model, with 299 bhp. As if that wasn't meaty enough, AMG then add four high-lift cams, four valves per cylinder, and thus increase the bhp by a massive 25 per cent. The engine bay, incidentally, has to be enlarged to accommodate such a huge engine. The suspension is improved, additions being shorter coil springs, and Bilstein dampers; the alloy wheels are then added with ultra-low-profile Pirelli DT88s.

That's all well and good, you may be thinking, but what sort of performance does all this work produce? Well, when *Motor* magazine tested the car in January 1987, it was the fastest automatic car ever to have passed through their hands (with the exception of Andromeda, a 1000 bhp hot rod Model T). Jeff's AMG 560 E will out-accelerate a Ferrari Testarossa, a Porsche 911 Turbo, and almost anything else, beating them all the way up the scale with figures of 0–60 mph in 5 seconds dead, and 0–100 in 12.6. *Motor* ceased recording its top speed at 164 mph, which had not taken it all the way, but was getting too close for comfort.

Is Jeff pleased with his car? I don't know—I never seem to be able to catch him.

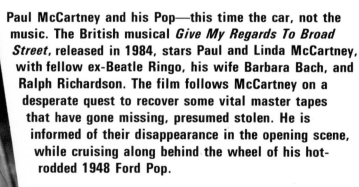

Paul McCartney and his Pop—this time the car, not the music. The British musical *Give My Regards To Broad Street*, released in 1984, stars Paul and Linda McCartney, with fellow ex-Beatle Ringo, his wife Barbara Bach, and Ralph Richardson. The film follows McCartney on a desperate quest to recover some vital master tapes that have gone missing, presumed stolen. He is informed of their disappearance in the opening scene, while cruising along behind the wheel of his hot-rodded 1948 Ford Pop.

The dragstrip-style Pop was built in the UK by Geoff Cousins, and is powered by a 3.5-litre Rover V8 which, along with the transmission, takes up so much room that the driver's seat is now located where the back one used to be. The car is finished in black lacquer and complemented by tri-coloured candy flames. The interior is Art Deco style, with a headlining that the production company air-brushed to look like leather! It also comes complete with telephones which play a vital role in the script.

Although Paul had the car during filming, it was later given away by MTV. As is often the problem with car competitions of this sort, the winners, twin sisters, had no interest in cars at all—which is just as well really, because they were too young to get insured anyway! You win some, you lose some.

An appetite whetter. This 1959 Maserati TIPO 61, more commonly known as the Birdcage, indicates the standards that can be expected from the rest of Nick Mason's collection

Nick Mason

Nick in the driving seat, this time behind the wheel of his beloved 1935 Aston Martin Ulster

Nick Mason describes himself as a racing enthusiast. However, I would describe him as a man obsessed with racing. This may seem a strong word to use, but it fits. Nick owns a huge collection of racing cars, which almost span the history of the track, from 1901 to the present day. But a collector he is not; he's a competitor, and can regularly be spotted out on the track, be it Silverstone, Le Mans, or Mosport Park in Canada.

Nick, who is more commonly recognized as the drummer with the hugely successful band Pink Floyd, has been interested in racing since his early childhood. His father, Bill Mason, recognized for his motor sport documentaries, was a keen amateur racer, who owned and raced a beautiful 4.5-litre vintage Bentley. Nick has fond memories of huddling in the back, hiding under the tonneau cover for warmth, as the Bentley ferried them to and from Silverstone and other circuits. Together he, his father and friend Wally Saunders (an ex-Bentley team mechanic) would, on arrival, strip the Bentley of as much weight as possible to prepare it for racing. That included exchanging the standard windscreen for the much lighter Brooklands type. It was Nick's first taste of the track and it made an impression that was to dominate the rest of his life. The Bentley now forms part of his vast collection, with his father ensuring that it still gets out on those country roads every summer.

Top right Nick's 1954 Grand Prix 250F Maserati parked up in France

Top One of its stablemates is this black 512S Ferrari

Centre Then there's the 250 GTO, commonly known as the Berlinetta

Bottom The list goes on—this time it's a Lola T297, raced by Nick and sponsored by his record company. It is painted in 'The Wall' graphics, in acknowledgement of Pink Floyd's phenomenally successful album and film

Right This 1936 B-type ERA was purchased by Nick in 1980. The 1938 Grand Prix winner is known as R10B

Nick's first car was a 1928 Austin 7, from which he learnt the rudiments of mechanics—there wasn't much choice, it was either sit at the side of the road or get out a spanner. An A7 'Chummy' also appears in Nick's collection as the sole sentimental vehicle, all of its stablemates being geared to race. Following the A7 came a 1930 Aston Martin International which heralded the start of a lifelong fascination with pre-war Astons, a relationship that would eventually culminate in Nick's formation of Mortane Engineering who now, in partnership with Derrick Edwards, are the biggest pre-war A M specialists in the world.

The year 1975 saw the arrival of a 1935 Aston Martin Ulster—and the start of his racing career, which is almost as varied as his cars. The Aston/Mason relationship has seen Nick and the 1935 Ulster take a vast majority of the British track records for pre-war vehicles, including Brands Hatch, Oulton Park and Silverstone. He has also been two times winner of the Itala trophy, one of the most prestigious awards for vintage car racing; he was driving his Bugatti 35B, which he also drove to victory at the Nürburgring in 1984, winning his class with an average speed of just over 107 mph. In addition to this, behind the wheel of his 1957 Grand Prix Maserati 250F, Nick won his class in the Historic Sports Car Club Championships.

He has also become a regular at Le Mans, first appearing in 1979. At the invitation of Dorset Racing Associates, he drove a Lola T297 in the Group 6 2-litre class. He and his two co-drivers, Richard Jenvey and Brian Joscelyne, finished second in the class, won the Index of Performance and finished 18th overall. A commendable first result. Nick then returned, again competing in the DRA Lola, coming third in class, and in 1982 appeared driving a BMW M1. The following year, co-driving with Chris Craft and Elisio Salazer, he competed in a Japanese Dome Group C car. Then, in 1984, he drove the Canon 956 Porsche with Rene Metge and Richard Lloyd in the 24-hour race.

In 1984, Nick drove another Porsche 956 in two other races, the Silverstone 1000 km race and at Mosport Park in Canada. On both occasions his Rothmans car was also used as the official camera vehicle.

And so to the famous collection. It comprises, as you would expect, a selection of pre-war Astons, including both the 1935 Ulster and 1930 International team car, LM7; there is also a 1970 Ferrari 512S, a 365 GTB/4 (more commonly known as the Daytona), a 250 GTO (the Berlinetta), a Lancia Stratos, the Bugatti and Bentley already mentioned, a 1955 D-type Jaguar, the 1957 Grand Prix Maserati 250F, a type 61 Maserati, a 1979 McLaren M29, a Tyrrell 008, together with a smattering of other Formula cars. He also owns a 1901 Panhard which is the oldest car in his collection.

Nick Mason is certainly the most involved of all our featured celebrities: he owns, races and restores a collection of cars that is almost unrivalled in its comprehensiveness. His collection is a true reflection of Nick's total involvement and dedication to the sport he has loved since childhood. A documentary has recently been made about Nick's life behind the drumset and behind the wheel. The half-hour film provides an understanding view of his two great passions in life, and has a very apt title: *Life Could Be A Dream*.

The date 26 January 1925 seems too ordinary a beginning for such an extraordinary man. Paul Newman is, quite simply, brilliant at what he does, be it making movies or racing cars. Newman's ability on the silver screen has been recognized throughout the world, a 33-year career with the world's box offices at his feet and countless classics under his belt will prove that; but what of his driving ability? Many view Newman's obsession with the track as a part-time hobby and not a passion stemming

Paul Newman

from a genuine ability to race. However, ask those who have competed in recent SCCA championships, who have seen the blue and white Nissan flash past, and they will tell you a different story.

The Sports Car Club of America GT-1 and Trans Am Series are Newman's latest interest, and their championships his goal. He rarely fails at what he does, and if he ever does lose these days, it's generally more to do with the inevitable problems relating to highly-tuned performance engines than a reflection of his ability. That's not to say that his GTO Nissan hasn't served him well; when the going's good, Newman and his 300ZX are almost always expected to set new track records, and winning the SCCA championships, which he has for the past two years, is becoming a matter of course. About his racing, Newman says: 'It's part of the allure, I guess, to kick the bejesus out of the young Turks. I have had some hairy moments. But Joanne trusts me.'

Newman's fascination with the automobile first came to the public's attention in 1969, when Universal Pictures released a highly auto-orientated film, with a title that said it all: *Winning*. Co-starring with his wife, Joanne Woodward, Newman played an enthusiast who would let nothing come between him and the track. *Winning* was a success, though not a blockbuster, but by this time Newman had four Oscar nominations for Best Actor under his belt, his most recent being *Cool Hand Luke* in 1967; that was enough to draw a crowd, whether they were interested in the car angle or not. Newman had done his research, and undergone a high-performance driving course in preparation for filming. He had also participated in a celebrity race to inaugurate the official opening of the Ontario Motor Speedway. Oh, and filmed *Butch Cassidy And The Sundance Kid*, too. A busy year in anyone's book, but especially relevant to ours. Paul Newman had caught the driving bug.

In 1972, three years after Newman had undergone his performance driving course, he was out on the track participating in regional races behind the wheel of a Datsun, a partnership which has so far lasted 15 years. A year later, in 1973, while *The Sting* launched itself on the movie world, Newman was busy qualifying for the SCCA championships, and by 1976 he had won his first SCCA national road-racing title, running a TR-6 in the D Production class. In 1978 he cemented a relationship that had started, and faltered, back in 1974, by driving a 280Z and 200SX Datsun for the Bob Sharp Racing Team, of which he is now a partner. The year 1979 saw Newman collect two North-East divisional crowns—B Sedan and C Production classes—winning 14 out of 16 races. He also drove a Porsche 935 at Le Mans and won his second SCCA national championship.

The early 1980s saw him elbowing his way into, and up through, the GT-1 and Trans Am Series. In 1982, which must rate as one of his most memorable years, he defeated what looked like an overwhelming professional field in the Minnesota Trans Am heat; at the same time, movie-goers all over the world were applauding him for his performance in *The Verdict*, for which he received his sixth Academy Award nomination, having missed the Oscar once again the previous year in *Absence Of Malice*. Ten new track records, and his third national championship, came in 1985, while 1986 saw a second consecutive GT-1 title. Then in 1987 he finally won the Oscar for Best Actor in *The Color Of Money*, an award that had eluded him since 1958 when he was first nominated for *Cat On A Hot Tin Roof*.

Those who sneered at Newman's acting ability, putting it down to his boyish good looks, have had to bite their tongues as he has matured into one of Hollywood's finest actors; those who scoffed at his racing fetish and put it down to his money and influential status have also bitten their tongues. He just keeps on winning.

Newman also raced successfully to second place in the 1979 24 Heures du Mans in this Hawaiian Tropic-sponsored Porsche 935

Previous page Paul Newman's current championship ride is shared with co-driver Jim Fitzgerald in this 1968 Nissan 300ZX. For SCCA events the car uses a turbocharged 2.8-litre V6 but for the IMSA GTO series they use a turbo's 3-litre V6. In SCCA form it produces 550 bhp (*Inset* Newman tries Needham's Rocket Car for size)

He is also involved with an Indianapolis car campaigned by Carl Hass and Mario Andretti, but here he's having some fun in something a little less serious

Photo : Rex Features Ltd

David Lee Roth, ex-lead singer with the rock group Van Halen, is, fortunately for us, an exhibitionist. From his mane of blonde hair to his vividly coloured clothes, you can tell that he needs to be noticed. A red and white 1951 Convertible Mercury is the perfect vehicle for such a desire. Nobody could ever call it subtle—stunning yes, subtle, no.

This beautiful Merc belongs to an élite group of early 1950s cars where looks are what counts—it's a lead sled. The name was originally adopted to signify that the car's bodywork had been smoothed out in good-old-fashioned lead, not by the new synthetic fillers; it now means just two things: low, and seriously slow. Who wants to race by when the world is willing to stand and stare?

Mr Roth's Mercury is certainly one of the finest examples of a lead sled—the '49 to '51 Mercs being the sledders' favourites, beating their contemporaries such as the other Fords, the Chevys and the Buicks. Roth's '51 obviously didn't require the compulsory roof chop, but the suspension was lowered by 4 in. to give it the necessary sled-stance. Other modifications include the addition of a De Soto grille—the only part of a De Soto worth having; Appleton spotlights; beautiful chrome lake pipes and wheels; plus white-wall tyres, which finish off the all-round effect.

The Merc and its conspicuous driver can be seen cruising the streets of Hollywood on most sunny days. With the V8 rumbling, it glides past, seeming to hover inches above the ground. When heads turn, which they invariably do, David Lee Roth knows he is driving the right car—you just *have* to take a second look.

David Lee Roth

Photo : Neal Preston /LFI © 1987 AI LFI Ltd

Brian Setzer

When it comes to knowing about the good things in life, Brian Setzer is an expert. Ex-lead singer with the Stray Cats, he now basks in the American sunshine, having left England and its infamous weather behind him. Setzer has always been a fan of the 1950s; being a successful rock musician has meant that he can realize his dream and drive the fabulous beasts of an era long gone.

His first-ever car was a pink '57 Chevy. At present his daily driver is a yellow and black '56 Bel Air, with colour co-ordinated interior. His other cars, used less frequently, are enough to make you head for the nearest guitar shop in search of the success and lifestyle that Brian now enjoys.

To start with there's the wickedly chopped '51 Mercury that was used in *American Graffiti*.

The Mercury is, however, not Setzer's favourite possession; he likes his car's acceleration to be as impressive as the bodywork, and acceleration is something that Mercs, like all lead sleds, simply do not have. Basically, he needed a hot rod; enter the '34 three-window Ford. The engine is a 350 cu. in. small-block Chevy with Holley carb, which supplies enough brake horsepower to keep Setzer happy. He also owns a chopped and channelled 1931 coupé that was pictured on the Cats' 'Rant 'n' Rave' album cover. Oh, and I mustn't forget the custom '53 Harley-Davidson.

When Setzer bought the Merc it was far from immaculate, as it was only ever treated to a cosmetic cover-up for the film, and was used afterwards as a *Graffiti* exhibit at Universal Studios. Once purchased, it was sent off to Ed 'Big Daddy' Roth's workshop where it was painted and striped. Mr Roth, one of the world's most respected customizers, also added a very personal touch on the left rear quarter, which reads 'Runaway Boy'; a nice reminder of one of the Stray Cats' most popular singles, and a very appropriate description of the driver.

Taking all the cars into consideration, Brian Setzer must own one of the most comprehensive collections of 1950s imagery on four wheels. The fins and the chrome come in the shape of his Bel Air, the Mercury represents the low-and-slow lead sleds, and the '31 and '34 neatly take care of the hot rods. He's got the whole set and, of course, the sunshine. That's what I meant when I said he understood the good things in life.

Above Sylvester Stallone sits astride his beautiful Harley-Davidson with its personalized Italian Stallion gas tank

Below The latest addition to Stallone's stable is this black 500 SEC Mercedes, modified by Koenig, the prestigious West German customizers

In 1976, Sylvester Stallone hit the big time. *Rocky*, a film he both starred in and wrote, won an Oscar for Best Picture. It also catapulted Mr Stallone to superstardom and overshadowed his brief appearance in another 1976 release, *Cannonball*—not to be confused with *The Cannonball Run* series of films, although similar in content. *Cannonball* was the first hint that Stallone was a keen car enthusiast.

While the career of Rocky Balboa was fed, sequel by sequel, to cinema-goers worldwide, Stallone was developing more and more of an interest in fast luxury sports cars. Little opportunity arose to feature any such cars in the four Rockys, nor were any likely to flash through the jungles of *First Blood* and its follow-up. But, if you watch *Rocky IV* closely, you will notice two Lamborghinis sitting in Balboa's driveway. Both the red Countach and the black Jalpa were gifts from Lamborghini and, I guess, by way of thanks, Stallone included them in his film. They took the place of a black Koenig Mercedes which was scheduled to appear, having just joined Stallone's personal collection of impressive automobiles.

This shot from Stallone's most car-orientated film to date, *Cobra*, shows the customizers' favourite car, the 1949 Mercury

Stallone plays a street-wise cop named Marion Cobretti (aka Cobra), who, while on the trail of psychopaths and mass-murderers, must protect his model girlfriend Ingrid, played by Brigitte Nielsen (aka Mrs Stallone). Although the film appears to contain only one Merc, it was necessary to build four to perform various different tasks. One was needed as a 'clean cruiser' for close-up shots; two were stunt cars, one required to smash through a building and ultimately catch fire, and the other to do some incredible jumps and 360-degree spins (an ample excuse for the full roll-cage); and finally a back-up 'cruiser'. With film production costs running so high, and schedules so tight, many studios now believe that if any car plays a vital role in filming, it is better to have an understudy at the ready, just in case.

All the Mercs were built by Eddie Paul in Los Angeles, and they were all de-chromed, nosed and decked 1950 models. A 2 in. roof chop and tunnelled tail-lights completed the body modifications. The colour, grey metallic, was apparently chosen because fake blood shows up best on a grey background—but then, you must never believe all that you read. Power for all the Mercs was supplied by small-block Chevys, although the 'cruiser', already treated to a superior paint-job for those close-up shots, also received more bhp. The additions, which gave it 30 per cent more power, consisted of a blower and nitrous oxide (otherwise known as laughing gas!). With a top speed of 140 mph, an oxide-assisted 0–60 time of a dumbfounding 4 seconds, the Merc supplied any power that *Cobra* may well have been lacking.

The Koenig was the first of its kind to leave the stables of these prestigious West German supercar modifiers. The engine, based on the original 500 SEC, comes complete with a Paxton supercharger, gives 320 bhp, has a top speed of 265 km/h, and accelerates from 0–100 km/h in 5.5 seconds—it's quick! The exterior is completely black, complemented by the beautiful palomino leather interior. The Koenig Mercedes was delivered to Stallone in March 1985 and is, apparently, one of his regular 'drivers'. He must be impressed with their work. By the beginning of 1988, Stallone will be behind the wheel of his second Koenig 'special', a 710 bhp Turbo Testarossa.

Several Mercurys appear in various sections of this book, and each time the rule of thumb is that these fat Fords simply do not go fast. Here is the exception to the rule. *Cobra*, released in 1986, is Sylvester Stallone's most auto-orientated movie to date. Although not a great box-office success, *Cobra* featured some superb stunts involving a stunning 1950 Mercury.

Photo : Ross Marino/LFI © 1987 Al LFI Ltd

Eddie Van Halen, lead guitarist with the rock group Van Halen, is the proud owner of this wonderful 1964 Volkswagen. The Beetle has been subtly customized according to a style that originated alongside the beaches of Southern California. The style, that has now spread worldwide, is called simply Cal-look, in honour of its birthplace, and the principle is simple: clean it up and drop it down. To 'clean up' a Volkswagen all the peripheral items, such as chrome trim, should be removed, thus improving the VW's already smooth shape. Cal-lookers are 'dropped down' by adjusting the front suspension—the lower, as Eddie's '64 demonstrates, the better.

Louie White of Reseda, California, smoothed out Van Halen's Bug by removing almost all of the chrome, including the bonnet handle, emblem and door trim. He also removed the indicators from the front wings—flashing sidelights within the main headlamp unit now suffice. The VW, being owned by a musician, had to sound as good as it looked, and with the addition of a 1914 cc tuned engine and a Fourtuned muffler exhaust system, it does.

The final touches, including the fitting of European-style bumpers (no unsightly overriders), gleaming Porsche alloy wheels and a stunning dark-grey metallic enamel finish, have made Van Halen's li'l Bug one of the subtlest and cheapest (at $8000) cars in this book. It also happens to be one of the best.

Andrew Ridgeley

Everybody crashes cars. It is not, as the media would have us believe, a habit peculiar to the rich and famous. One of the problems of being a celebrity with an interest in racing is, as Andrew Ridgeley of Wham! discovered, that if you fancy a few circuits of the track, the whole world waits with eager anticipation.

Racing in the Renault 5 Elf Turbo UK Cup was Ridgeley's first time behind the wheel in serious competition and, admittedly, he didn't do very well. The photographers, on the other hand, earned a small fortune, showing the world a few bumped and battered Renaults. Ridgeley drove a special 'celebrity car' in Renault's 11-race championship and therefore found himself in the tricky position of competing with 39 fully-experienced drivers, such as Bill McGovern, three-times British saloon car champion.

In 1986, while living in Monaco, Ridgeley competed in the French Formula 3 Championship and, seemingly more at home in a single-seater, finished as a middle-to-front runner. A great improvement on the previous year, which meant, of course, that nobody heard about it.

The California Kid

There are car films and then there are car films—and most auto enthusiasts would dismiss most of them because of their inherent mistakes. It is rare that a car fan can find nothing wrong, but a case in point is *The California Kid*.

This movie, made for TV in 1974, concerned a small-town sheriff who had a thing, mainly the reinforced bumper of his cruiser, against offenders. Anybody he caught speeding was enticed on to a tricky mountain road from which they never returned. Enter our hero, the California Kid, the hot-rodding brother of one of Sheriff Morrow's victims, played by Martin Sheen driving one of the best street rods ever to cross our screens.

The car in question was conceived and created by California hot rodder Pete Chapouris and is an original '34 Model 40 Ford three-window coupé. When Pete modified it in the early 1970s, he was really bucking the trend by

chopping the roof and painting it black 'n' flames, but his outrageous approach paid off with a starring part. Unfortunately, Pete had to stand by while the film crew tortured his car with constant slams of the door, 69 in all, spin-outs and potentially disastrous cliff-edge chases.

When the Kid arrives looking for his brother, played by Sheen's real-life brother Joe Estevez, he soon understands the sheriff's scheme and the fact that he was responsible for his brother's death. The Kid takes his car up into the mountain and practises until he is curve-perfect. He then entices the sheriff out on to the road, knowing that he, and not the sheriff, will be the one to come back—and that's exactly what happens.

As for the car, it survived but Pete sold it, only to realize his mistake and therefore having to pay an exorbitant price to get it back. He drove it constantly until 1986, when he sold it again.

61

There is only one car that can claim to be the reason for a best-selling thriller, and a great movie. It's a red and white 1958 Plymouth Fury, and it's called Christine.

Based on the book by top novelist Stephen King, the 1983 RCA/Columbia film *Christine* told the story of a Fury with demonic powers.

Christine is first seen in 1958, on the Plymouth production line, where she claims her first victim, an innocent Chrysler employee who gets in to turn her radio off, but he soon realizes his fatal mistake as the doors slam shut and his seat starts to move forwards, eventually crushing him to death against the steering wheel. Christine was 'Born To Be Bad', which was what the radio was playing all along.

The film then moves to 1978, when Arnie Cunningham spots her rusting away in a yard. He is inexplicably drawn towards the wreck, and eventually convinces the reluctant owner to part with her. It was the biggest mistake he ever made.

Christine begins to use her powers of seduction to ensure Arnie's total devotion, and he soon begins to develop the tell-tale signs of total obsession, similar to that of her previous owner. He is no longer an innocent teenager who's mad about Furys—he's a furious man, mad about anything, obsessed with his Fury.

In total, 17 different Plymouths were used in the making of the film, ranging from burnt-out wrecks, through mediocre runners, to two or three good cars, but there was only one pristine Christine, which was used for all the close-up shots. In one of the scenes, Christine has suffered several blows from a gang of high-school bullies with a sledgehammer, but once

Christine

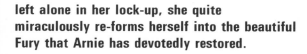

left alone in her lock-up, she quite miraculously re-forms herself into the beautiful Fury that Arnie has devotedly restored.

The special effects used in this scene are stunning, involving a complex and extremely expensive rubber moulding process. A special rubber compound was used, which was moulded into the shape of the car, then, once it had set, was sprayed to give it the appearance of metal. The car was then placed in a vacuum, and as the air was sucked out, the cameras rolled. The film was then simply reversed, giving the impression that the metal was pushing itself back into its original form.

It is interesting to note that in the book Christine is a four-door model—Stephen King was utilizing his artistic licence, as the 1958 Fury was only ever built with two doors.

The film is, if you're a fins fan, a pleasure to watch, and, whether you are or not, the special effects are brilliant.

Photos : © ITC Entertainment Ltd London W1A 1AG

F.A.B. Virgil. *Thunderbirds*, the incredibly successful Gerry Anderson production of 1966, had that very famous catchphrase. It also had a very famous car. F.A.B., by the way, was the trendy 1960s shortening for fabulous, and nothing more.

Lady Penelope's pink Rolls-Royce, named FAB 1, after its number plate, created something of a cult following. The Rolls possessed six wheels, and a clear roof which doubled as a retractable sun canopy. It was sprayed in a unique colour that had been specially created for Lady Penelope, and which was named, appropriately enough, Penelope Pink. Her faithful chauffeur Parker occupied the front seat, while Lady P sat in the back.

Although the body of FAB 1 had been lengthened, no extra passenger space was provided as most of the car was taken up by the massive engine, which was specified as being capable of over 300 mph; and then, of course, there were the four machine guns. The one most frequently used was hidden in the front radiator grille. The grille, a miniaturized version of a real Rolls-Royce one, had to be specially licensed by the prestigious company.

FAB 1, like the James Bond Lotus of later years, was also capable of aquatic travel. It could double as a hydrofoil, although this facility was only ever utilized in one episode.

A life-size replica of FAB 1 was built, obviously based on a real Rolls-Royce, that was identical to the miniature car, having six wheels and a body that had been lengthened by 4 ft. It was used for publicity purposes, with a look-alike Lady Penelope to add authenticity, but unfortunately has now totally disappeared. It was last seen in Buckinghamshire, England. Fans of FAB 1 have been trying to track it down ever since, so if you ever happen to see a bright pink Rolls-Royce with six wheels and a canopy, follow that car!

People like laughing at Volkswagens. In fact, it became such a worldwide hobby during the late 1960s that Doyle Dane & Bernbach, the New York advertising agency, used it as the basis for their incredibly successful VW ads. Some bright spark at Walt Disney also realized this, and came up with an idea for a film; a comedy about the day-to-day adventures of a little VW.

The Love Bug was released in 1969 and was an instant success, with both children and adults. Adults are, after all, only grown-up kids, and 12 million of them were chugging along behind the wheel of their very own potential Herbie.

In the first of Herbie's four adventures, he finds himself out on the track with his new owner, a small-time racing driver named Jim Douglas (played by Dean Jones). As Herbie takes the chequered flag time and again, watch out for the stream of beautiful ACs, Corvettes and Ferraris that fade into the distance as No. 53 goes hurtling past. Patrick Thorndyke, a jealous loser (played by Robert Stevenson),

checks the engine, not believing that this little VW could be capable of such speeds. What he finds is an innocent 1200 cc VW motor; although in reality, he was right—all the wheelieing and wheel-spinning was actually powered by Porsche.

About 30 Beetles, ranging from 1966 to 1969 models, were required for the various *Love Bug* stunts, which is a little confusing because the exterior of Herbie is very definitely pre-1967. Anyway, much of the special modification work required was carried out at the Wolfsburg factory in West Germany.

The number of Herbie's crazy antics is astonishing. From the two-wheel stunt driving (both rear and side); to the car lurching around, tyres heading in all directions, apparently drunk on Irish coffee (Thorndyke's doing); and, ultimately, to Herbie splitting in half at the end of the final race, the rear section over-taking the front portion to win, leaving the front half to come third.

Herbie

As if all that was not enough, Wolfsburg had to make Herbie appear to be driving unaided. For this, a driver, hidden by lace curtains, sat right in the back of the car, his foot pedals being just behind the front seats, the rear bench seat having been removed. This enabled side and brief frontal shots to be taken with the car appearing to drive itself. The chief pilot could also, with the aid of a fork-lift hydraulic system, a carbon-dioxide bottle and a powerful electric motor, operate 26 levers and buttons which, among other things, opened and shut all the doors, apparently without human hand.

The hydraulic Herbie was also used in some of the other *Love Bug* sequels. But *Herbie Rides Again*, *Herbie Goes To Monte Carlo* and *Herbie Goes Bananas* also featured new stunts, which demanded more special VWs to be constructed. Nobody is really sure how many Beetles were used throughout the Herbie series, although the original now proudly stands in the VW factory.

A car masterminded by computer, that is capable of 0–60 mph in 2 seconds (with booster assistance); that covers a standing quarter of a mile in 4.286 seconds, at a terminal speed of 300 mph; that brakes from 70–0 mph in 14 ft (with the assistance of retractable side fins); that has a turning circle of 2 ft (with rocket assistance); that has a surveillance scanner (which can detect anything happening anywhere) in its nose; and that runs on a hitherto-unheard-of engine—Knight Industries' turbojet with modified afterburners.

In the wrong hands, a car of these specifications could annihilate the world as we know it. In the right hands, at an estimated cost of $11,400,000, it could be the crime-fighting car of the century. Fortunately for us, it belongs to Knight Industries Two Thousand (hence the car's name, KITT), an organization set up to rid the streets of those who operate on the wrong side of the law.

Unfortunately for Bill Shelley, a stunt driver for Universal Studios, those remarkable specifications are totally fictitious. He sits behind the wheel of a black 1982 Pontiac and has the unenviable task of getting a regular Trans Am to perform the amazing feats that, were KITT fact and not fiction, would be everyday occurrences. A special 'jump' car is used for the various leaps necessary to block the path of escaping villains. This stunt car is equipped with a full roll-cage, heavy-duty shock absorbers, a strengthened chassis and special brakes. It also weighs only 1500 lb and can therefore fly off a compression ramp that Shelley constructed, and soar for approximately 25 ft before smashing back down to reality.

Reality is a highly-successful television series called *Knight Rider*, now in its sixth year of production. Neither *Knight Rider* nor KITT, now in convertible form, look like they're about to run out of fuel.

The Pink Panther, parked in a moment's tranquility, away from the gaping mouths and wide eyes that accompany it everywhere. It was built by Californian customizer Jay Ohrberg for the TV show of the same name. The latter opens with some lucky little blonde kid cruising along the boulevard driving this outrageous pinkmobile; he pulls up, the gullwing doors swing open and out sleuths the rinky-dink Panther. It was one of the first experiments to mix live action with animation, and what a success—the programmes are still being shown around the world.

Sadly the only action the car sees these days is at international car shows; however, Jay originally built the Pink Panther to run, as

The Pink Panther

those opening sequences clearly show. It is powered by a 500 horsepower Oldsmobile Toronado engine transposed from its original front-wheel-drive location to a rear-wheel-drive position thus giving that blonde kid somewhere to sit.

The carpeted 'pleasure capsule' entered through those gullwing doors contains a television set, for watching the Pink Panther of course, a soda fountain, natch, and matching pink cushions.

If you've ever wondered what's bright pink, 26 ft long, and makes people stare, you know the answer.

Over recent years it seems that the film studios have at last realized that there is a large proportion of the cinema-going public who enjoy spotting the odd interesting car flitting across the silver screen. Even if it is not of major importance, a cameo role by a beautiful car definitely adds to the enjoyment. Also, the right cars parked up in the background can instantly set the date, the location, and the mood.

Absolute Beginners and *Little Shop Of Horrors*, both recent muscials and both, oddly enough, filmed in England, are good examples of this.

Absolute Beginners was based on Colin McInnes' outstanding book of the same name. Set in London in the late 1950s, the film stars Eddie O'Connell and Patsy Kensit as teenage lovers growing up in a city apparently teeming with bitterness and greed. Lionel Blair plays a band manager who gains publicity by driving his newly-signed protégé around in a white '57 Chevy.

Little Shop Of Absolute Horrors'

Little Shop Of Horrors is set on Skid Row, *circa* 1960. It follows the budding relationship of a boy and a girl, with interference from a man-eating plant! The film is an unusual mixture: part musical, part horror, and part comedy—the latter provided by Steve Martin, playing a sadistic dentist who rides a Harley-Davidson.

To help make Pinewood Studios' set in England seem like Downtown USA, a bunch of 1950s fins were rounded up. The result is that,

throughout the film, V8s can be heard chugging down side alleys, while glints of chrome flash and then fade as a remarkable collection of automobiles cruise past in all directions.

It is, of course, unlikely that immaculate red, blue or white Chevys—all, in theory, less than three years old—would have been circling Downtown USA, or the streets of London, but I don't hear anyone complaining.

73

American Graffiti

A yellow 1932 Ford, a black 1955 Chevrolet, a white 1958 Impala and a maroon 1951 Mercury: these are the unlikely stars of *American Graffiti*, the cult movie released in 1973 that was directed by George Lucas. They quite simply stole the show, taking the limelight away from budding actors Richard Dreyfuss and Harrison Ford. They even managed to detract attention from the brilliantly perceptive screenplay which, set in 1962, centred around a bunch of 'pedal to the metal' kids who were learning to cope with life after graduation. No one can deny that they were, and will remain, a very special bunch of cars.

The hero of the film, although originally scripted to be Steve Milner, played by Paul Le Mat, turned out to be Milner's car, a certain little yellow '32. The five-window Deuce coupé was bought by Gary Kurtz, the producer, for $1300 from a selection that he had located before filming, mainly because it already had a chopped roof. Once purchased, the Deuce had its front fenders removed and the rear ones bobbed. The grille was sectioned, which entails literally cutting out a section in the middle and welding the top and bottom back together, thus shortening it. The bodywork was then totally stripped, and repainted in canary-yellow lacquer. The engine it ran on during filming was a 283 cu. in. Chevy V8. Chrome headers, a Man-A-Free inlet manifold and four 2G Rochester carbs gave the engine some sparkle.

The beautiful exterior, that launched a thousand project hot rods, is sadly like an ageing movie star's make-up: underneath, it's a totally different story. So long as the cameras don't pick them up, the unseen parts can be as tatty as hell. The coupé, like all tired-out old movie stars, created its fair share of trouble, which included proving almost impossible to attach any cameras to, and it also ran over the assistant cameraman!

The co-starring '58 Impala was bought, again by Kurtz, primarily for its red and white tuck-and-roll interior—the fact that this would be almost non-evident in the film does not seem to have bothered him. The Impala ran a 348 cu. in. engine and was treated to a new coat of paint in preparation for its silver-screen début. A set of chrome-reverse wheels were fitted, and a set of six '59 Cadillac bullet-shaped tail-lights were glued to the original lights.

Next comes the '51 Merc, which was purchased after it was found in the spectators' parking lot of a stock-car track—so again, don't expect wonders! With the exception of a quick roof chop, a shaved hood, trunk and doors, a one-bar grille and frenched headlights, the car was left almost as standard. The engine, as with most lead sleds, is stock.

Then there's the '55. Its history is certainly the longest of the four. While the others were lazing about in parking lots, this little Chevy was busy clocking up its first screen appearance in *Two-Lane Blacktop*, an earlier Gary Kurtz car movie. Its basic condition and specifications during filming were a little more impressive than the other three, as the preparation work was far more thorough. For a start, the car runs with some real power on a 454 cu. in. big-block. The Chevy was almost totally rebuilt, inside and out; hand-built front frame rails were fitted, plus a tube-axle suspended on Koni coil-over shock absorbers, and Airheart disc brakes were responsible for bringing it to a halt. The '55 was definitely streets ahead of its co-stars when it came to power and overall condition. However, it still fared no better when all four were put up for sale once *Graffiti* was in the can.

Advertisements ran in the Northern Californian local papers, and none of the cars attracted any buyers, except for the Impala which sold for the ridiculous sum of $200! Even though the Deuce was advertised at a mere $1500, people were just not interested. Once *American Graffiti* hit the streets, people changed their minds and money changed hands. The Merc, by the way, now belongs to ex-Stray Cat Brian Setzer, who is featured on pages 52–55.

The coupé, on the other hand, was not re-advertised—I guess the movie moguls figured one chance was enough. It ended up sitting for five years as an uncared-for exhibit at Universal Studios. In 1979, however, it was treated to a quick coat of paint and was hauled out to make an appearance in *More American Graffiti*. Both the run of the film (a pointless sequel) and the run of the Deuce, its engine now nearly seized, were short-lived. After filming, the little '32 found itself once again back at Universal, with the future looking bleak. Eventually, Steve Fitch, a keen *Graffiti* enthusiast, convinced the moguls to sell and took the Deuce home—where he also had the original Chevy. The reunion ended when Rich Figari, who was absolutely obsessed with the '32, convinced Fitch to sell. He had been 'phoning him almost fortnightly for $3\frac{1}{2}$ years! A delighted Rich took the coupé off to its present home in San Francisco.

All four cars are now lovingly cared for by devoted owners, so we can rest assured that none of these old movie stars will be forgotten.

Above One of the '55 Chevys used in *Graffiti* came to a bad end as a result of an illegal drag race

The black Chevy used in *American Graffiti* was actually constructed from the parts of two different '55s used in *Two-Lane Blacktop*. Released in 1971, two years earlier than *Graffiti*, the film followed the trail of a lone Chevy racing a Pontiac GTO across the southwest of America.

This classic film, almost surreal in quality, revolves totally around the race, emphasizing this by dispensing with any names, the characters being known simply as The Driver (played by singer/songwriter James Taylor), The Mechanic (Dennis Wilson of the Beach Boys) and GTO (Warren Oates).

A total of three Chevys were required for filming, two identical in case of breakdown

Left After sitting neglected at Universal Studios, the Pharaoh's Merc from *American Graffiti* is now in the caring hands of Brian Setzer

and a third 'stunt' '55 that was to be used in a crash scene which eventually did not take place. The two main Chevys were meticulously built by Richard Ruth (who also played a small part in the film) of Competition Engineering. A misunderstanding had taken place; Ruth thought he was supposed to be constructing two high-power, high-class machines, when in fact, what the producers wanted were two 'cosmetic' Chevys, quality being of little importance. Ruth even sprayed them in powder-blue lacquer, only to see his work painted over with grey primer—to create a realistic 'ready-to-race' hot rod look.

By the end of filming, both cars had suffered the normal heavy usage associated with films and were much the worse for wear, which is why parts from both were used to make the one good *Graffiti* car. The third, as yet unemployed, stunt car eventually got a job in the final crash scene of *Graffiti*.

Photos courtesy of Golden Communications

Japanese technology and a bit of film fantasy thrust this little Mitsubishi and its two eager Cannonballers into serious overdrive

Whatever the critics might say, if you like exotic sports cars, and you also enjoy the odd bit of celebrity spotting, *The Cannonball Run* is enjoyable entertainment. Released in 1981, at a time when trans-American road-racing films were all the rage, it received by far the most attention simply because of the plethora of famous faces.

Admittedly the plot was a bit of a farce. Sammy Davis, Jr. and Dean Martin try to foil the cops and avoid speeding tickets by masquerading as nuns (in a Ferrari?!); Farrah Fawcett-Majors, a tree lover, gets kidnapped by Burt Reynolds and drugged up to the eyeballs by a deranged doctor; Peter Fonda appears in an unlikely role as the leader of a biking gang; Roger Moore is an eccentric Englishman abroad, who drives an Aston Martin and thinks he's James Bond; and Burt Reynolds' mechanic (Dom DeLuise) has an alter-ego called Captain Chaos—which is the eventual reason for them losing the race, as he forces Reynolds to stop inches away from the finish line so that he can rush to the aid of a drowning cat.

The Cannonball Run

Roger Moore makes a hasty exit from his Aston Martin DB6 as he goes for the cigar lighter and hits the wrong button

It is easy to deprecate such antics, but Hal Needham, the director, took part in the real, and highly illegal, coast-to-coast run of '79, and script writer Brock Yates actually organized it. I wasn't there, and I don't know anyone who was, so it could possibly have been just like the film, but I doubt it.

Cannonball Run II, which was released three years later, in 1984, again starred Burt Reynolds as head Cannonballer, with guests including Frank Sinatra and Shirley MacLaine, and was almost identical in content. Both *The Cannonball Run* and *Cannonball Run II* should not be viewed seriously—to think any of the actors really thought they were making a great movie is probably more foolish than the script. They should both be treated as a privileged insight into what some of the biggest names in showbiz enjoy doing most in their spare time—having fun, being with a bunch of friends, and driving fast cars. In fact, it looks like they had a Ball.

SPEED
LIMIT
155

HAWAIIAN TROPIC

Some people just never know when to quit. The
driver of this fenderless Porsche is determined not
to be left by the wayside. He's back on the road,
and back in the race

A dusty highway stretching as far as the eye can see. The horizon wavering in the scorching midday sun. In the cab of a massive rumbling truck the air-conditioning hums quietly, occasionally interrupted by the spasmodic crackling of a CB. The driver's hands rest lackadaisically on the huge steering wheel, gently keeping the thundering beast on its course down a never-ending road. He daydreams, his thoughts as far away as his destination.

If those thoughts could be captured, and recorded on celluloid, it is probable that what you would have is Sam Peckinpah's *Convoy*. Released in 1978, this wonderfully improbable film stars Kris Kristofferson as a trucker named Martin Penwald, or Rubber Duck if you're on the end of a CB. The story follows Penwald's adventures after having been stopped for speeding by a bent cop named Lyle Wallace (Ernest Borgnine). Bribe taken, Wallace waves him on, only to give chase when he hears Rubber Duck bad-mouthing him across the air-waves. He catches him up at a truckstop which turns into a cloud of swirling dust and flying fists. The brawl ends with Wallace lying injured, as Penwald and his pals hit the road. The police alert goes out, and *Convoy* rolls into action.

The action-packed film continues with the trucking fraternity literally bulldozing a town called Truckers Hell, in an effort to rescue a jailed good buddy. The final scenes see a huge National Guardsman roadblock at the entrance to a bridge, set up by Wallace to stop Penwald in his tracks. Having witnessed the boys bulldoze their way through a town, he should have known better. Penwald puts his foot down, hurtles towards them, hits head on, his truck bursts into flames, crashes over the edge and into the river.

Peckinpah's direction must be commended, his influence made apparent by the wonderful cinematography throughout the film. If you wonder what happens to Penwald, just remember what his good buddies call him.

Few films can claim to have given such all-round entertainment as *Grease*. In fact, few modern musicals can claim to have given any pleasure at all; it is a fine art to produce a film punctuated with songs that actually enhance the atmosphere—it helps, of course, if the soundtrack is as good as *Grease*.

Based on the long-running Broadway show of the same name, *Grease*, released in 1978, was a box-office smash. Starring John Travolta and Olivia Newton-John as Danny and Sandy, the film follows their relationship which started on holiday where being cool didn't count. Danny wooed Sandy on the beaches, expecting never to see her again. He was wrong, of course. Sandy turns up for her first day at Rydell High, is befriended by The Pink Ladies, only to find that they go hand in hand with the T-Birds, and the number one T-Bird is Danny Zuko. He is, of course, no longer her romeo from the beach, he is Mr Cool; and she is no longer his Juliet, rather more Miss Naïve. But, as the song says, Grease is for Lovers, and it's obvious that, under all that Brylcreem, he is still Mr Right.

The film follows Rydell's class of '59 through dance contests, summer loving, drive-ins, and a race at Thunder Road. Enter the cars.

Greased Lightnin' is the T-Birds' dream car; it is also a 1947 Convertible Ford. All the cars used in *Grease*, even the 'back-drops', were built by Eddie Paul of Customs by Eddie in El Segundo, California. Eddie was given just two weeks to find, purchase and build 30 cars from the 1950s. In the script, Danny and his gang dream of owning a beautiful blood-red car they call Greased Lightnin', and they end up racing their rival gang, The Scorpions, in White Lightnin', which is in fact a nicer car. The Scorpions run in Hell's Chariot, a convertible Mercury, but more of that later.

Eddie, meanwhile, was busy scurrying around looking for a '47; he found what he says was literally a basket-case, picked up the bits and took it home. He proceeded to transform this into Greased Lightnin', then two days later, with that part of the film completed, Greased Lightnin' returned to his workshop where he reversed the whole process, turning it back into a jalopy, which is the wreck that you see Danny so proudly introduce as the T-Birds' new car; they, of course, just nod in disbelief. Then it was back to Eddie, who transformed it into White Lightnin', the beautiful machine the T-Birds race at Thunder Road. If you think Eddie had his work cut out, you're right—he had to conduct that whole process twice, preparing twin cars in case something went wrong with either of them, which would have been disastrous for the movie's schedule.

This, believe it or not, is Greased Lightnin', the 1947 Ford that starred in *Grease*. Eddie Paul of El Segundo took less than a week to transform this jalopy into the stunning hot rod that the T-Birds used to thrash the Scorpions at Thunder Road

We now see Eddie with his work literally cut out; he had had no success unearthing a convertible Mercury to star as the Scorpions' Hell's Chariot, so had settled for two hardtops (although he probably did have double vision by this time as it was again necessary to produce twin cars). In the time allowed, he had been lucky to find two hardtop Mercs, but there was certainly no way he would find two of the same year, so he settled for a '49 and a '50. Both needed only minor alterations to appear identical, which was lucky, because as I said, there was a lot to do. Both roofs had to be cut

off, and then the cars had to be finished to the extremely high standards demanded by the studio, with all the little extras like rotating blades attached to the hub caps that eventually ripped a hole right down the body of the '47, and of course those flames had to appear from the exhaust pipes in angry bursts.

Eddie managed to complete all 30 cars within the two weeks he was given. I guess when *Grease* went on to become one of the most popular films of the 1970s, he had the time to reflect that it had all been worth it.

The car-chase film to end all car-chase films was the aim of writer, producer, director H. B. 'Toby' Halicki's *Gone In 60 Seconds*—and it probably is, except that the plot is pretty improbable. Our hero, Maindrain Pace, played by Halicki, thinks stealing cars to order, hence the title, is a lot more rewarding (he has a $400,000 contract to fulfil) and a lot more fun than working in the family laboratory.

The problem arises when 48 cars have to be located, stolen and delivered to the docks in just five days. Pace and his team do the business except that 'Eleanor' (he code-names each car), a 1973 Mustang, proves harder to steal than he expected. Unaware that his brother Eugene has double-crossed him, Pace tries for the third time only to find the police waiting. Thus ensues one of the longest, at 40 minutes, chase sequences on celluloid. I won't tell you what happens in the end because that would spoil *Gone In 60 Seconds II*.

Gone in 60 Seconds

Heart Like A Wheel

Shirley Muldowney is a remarkable woman. She is the only driver, male or female, to have won three National Hot Rod Association World Championships. The sacrifices she made to become the NHRA's Top Fuel Champion were immense, as was her courage and determination. *Heart Like A Wheel* is her story.

Released in 1983, it stars Bonnie Bedelia as Muldowney, and Beau Bridges as Connie Kalitta—Shirley's sponsor, lover and, ultimately, her toughest competitor. The film follows her 25-year-long struggle to the top; her early encounters with Don 'Big Daddy' Garlits, a legend on the drag-racing straights; to her private life, an unsuccessful marriage, her confusing relationship with Kalitta, and her devotion to her son, who eventually became her number one mechanic.

Filmed at the Orange County Raceway in Southern California, the action is spectacular. The horrific accidents, sadly an acknowledged hazard of drag racing, are filmed with understanding and feeling, and not just as 'another great stunt'. *Heart Like A Wheel* provides a rare insight into the people who live in a world where the cars accelerate to over 250 mph in less than 6 seconds.

Mad Max

In a world laid to industrial ruin that has reverted to survival of the fittest, or fastest, where dusty horizons stretch as far as the eye can see and gang warfare has replaced law and order, there is only one way to keep safe—keep moving. A gallon of gas thus becomes imperative to survival; if you want some, it's quite simple, you kill for it.

This is the world into which Max (played by Mel Gibson) finds himself thrown. Previous moral codes and human decency lie in archaic ruin by the wayside. Max, following the death of his wife and children at the hands of a marauding gang, becomes the avenging angel of this frighteningly conceivable post-oil age. He quits his job as a highway patrol officer, but, smart cop that he is, remembers to take the patrol car. The baddies had better watch out— Max is getting mad, and he's also getting even.

His pursuit car, based on the Ford Falcon XA coupé, a model exclusive to Australia, the actual (though not intended) location of the films, was an instant success. The audience fantasized about being in his shoes—most of them having probably driven to the cinema in something not dissimilar. They were unlikely to have the on/off supercharger, though. But then neither did Max; his was a dummy powered by an electric motor. Real or not, the car is reputed to have cost 35,000 Australian dollars.

From *Mad Max*, released in 1981, through its sequel (actually better than the original) to *Mad Max Beyond Thunderdome*, Max's successful survival can be attributed to his determination, ingenuity and brilliant driving. The stunts throughout all three films are, as you would expect, superb, with some amazing leaps performed by vehicles that only just look safe enough to sit in.

Where is the Falcon now? Well, contrary to the impression given by *Mad Max II*, the car was not destroyed, and is at present touring the show circuits, receiving the sort of attention that confirms the phenomenal and continued success of the Mad Max series. What then lies beyond Thunderdome?

The most expensive car ever to be featured in a film must surely be the $1.5 million prototype that starred in the stylistic film *The Wraith*.

Charlie Sheen (see his dad on page 60) plays The Wraith, a spectral being whose death was caused by a gang of marauding American punks. He's back, he's angry, and he's gonna make them pay.

The prototype pace car, which plays the mysterious Turbo Interceptor, was built by the Dodge division of the Chrysler Corporation, and Pittsburgh Paint and Glass. It is built on a tube-frame chassis and is powered by the unique Chrysler 2.2-litre four-cylinder engine, which is fitted with a Cosworth 16-valve head and twin turbochargers; it is capable of speeds in the region of 200 mph—that's fact, not fiction!

The real pace car was not actually used in any action shots, but served as the close-up car,

while two identical bodies were mounted on dune-buggy chassis for stunt purposes. Four more were placed on empty frames which would be used in various crash sequences. Just to make sure no one on set decided to get in and take the pace car out for a spin, it arrived with its own driver, mechanic and bodyguard, compliments of Chrysler . . . .

The wonderful stunts featured in the film were designed and co-ordinated by Buddy Joe Hooker, a legend in the stunt world—he holds world records for, among other things, a rocket-assisted jump that he performed for the Burt Reynolds' movie *Hooper*.

With Buddy Joe keeping a watchful eye on the proceedings, the action simply has to be first-class. Watch out for cameo roles by a classic Corvette, a couple of tuned Trans Ams, a

The Wraith

Hannibal, Face, Murdock, and BA. They are The A Team—a hardened bunch of ex-Vietnam fighters who, wanted by the US Military Police, live life on the run. Their tactics of evasion are ingenious: Murdock pretends to be insane and subsequently ends up living in a mental asylum, and Hannibal makes good use of his ability as a master of disguise. They spend their time striving to put the world to rights, taking the law into their own hands in order to assist helpless victims of circumstance. If you need help, and you can find them, you can hire The A Team.

Each episode of this highly successful TV series, which has been running for over five years, sees The A Team restoring law and order in their own inimitable style. Their now infamous black Chevrolet van is used almost constantly in their war against the villains. BA Baracus, played by Mr T, is their ace mechanic—all he needs is a set of welding equipment, fortunately always to be found in whatever barn, shack or back lot they are hiding. He can transform the van into almost anything. In its five-year involvement with the show, the van has been armour-plated, smashed through roadblocks, used as a battering ram, and even doubled as a cannon, firing melons through a grain chute.

The A Team do have another means of transport, although used much less frequently, which is a red and white Corvette. Face, the most sophisticated of the four, usually drives it—when he's not being hurled about in the back of a certain black van.

The A Team

The Dodge Charger two-door hardtop sports
coupé produced between 1968 and 1970 was
the archetypal muscle car, the factory hot rod
to put all others on the trailer. It was
extremely powerful. By the end of its run it
was the Charger R/T and was powered by a
440 cu. in. Magnum V8 producing 375 hp. A
limited number of super-high-performance
Charger 500s were built for NASCAR racing,
some with Magnums and some with a 426
cu. in. hemi-head V8. The latter could run
almost 200 mph at Daytona.

Thankfully Dodge built an awful lot of regular
Chargers because the Dukes of Hazzard County,
Bo and Luke, have been using them up at a
phenomenal rate. The ones which get jumped
are specially strengthened to survive;
nevertheless, the producers have someone on
the road full-time buying Chargers which are
subsequently Generalized. That is, they are
given a liberal coating of orange paint, a
Confederate flag for the roof and a giant 01.

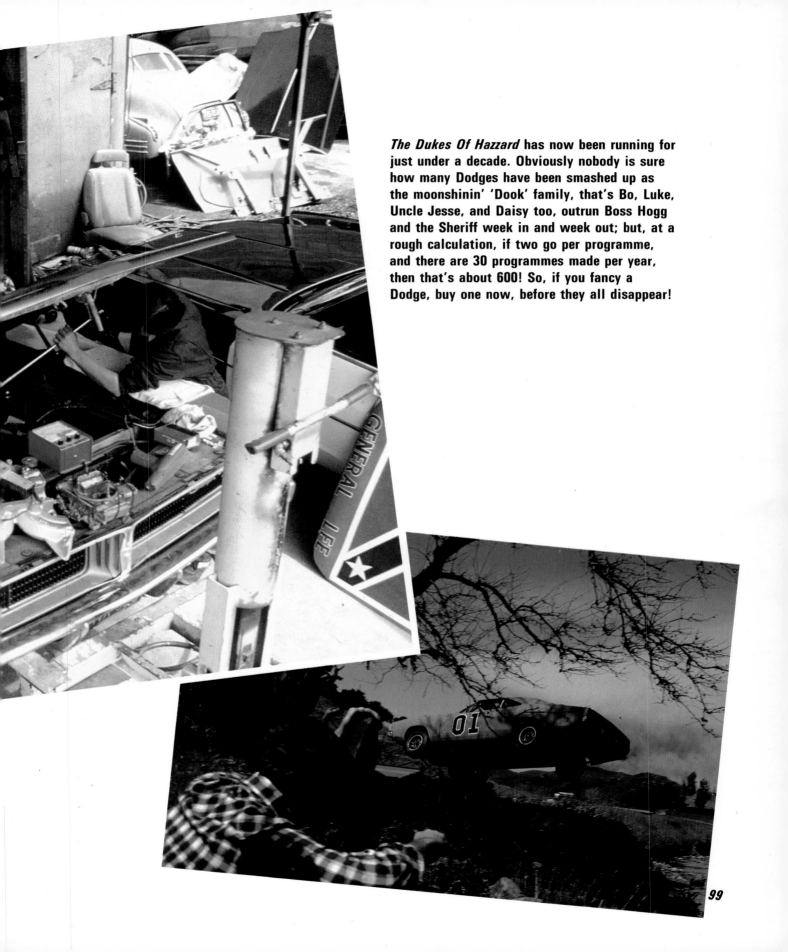

The Dukes Of Hazzard has now been running for just under a decade. Obviously nobody is sure how many Dodges have been smashed up as the moonshinin' 'Dook' family, that's Bo, Luke, Uncle Jesse, and Daisy too, outrun Boss Hogg and the Sheriff week in and week out; but, at a rough calculation, if two go per programme, and there are 30 programmes made per year, then that's about 600! So, if you fancy a Dodge, buy one now, before they all disappear!

Hardcastle & McCormick

Milton C. Hardcastle is an eccentric judge considering retirement, but, frustrated with a legal system that allows so many criminals to slip through legal loop-holes, he finds he cannot let go. He sees a way out of his dilemma when a known car thief, Mark McCormick, comes before him on the bench. He offers McCormick an alternative to life behind bars—parole, and a partnership.

Hardcastle (Brian Keith) and McCormick (Daniel Hugh-Kelly) join forces to become, with the judge's knowledge of the law, an unstoppable crime-busting duo. McCormick's talents as an ex-racing driver come in handy again and again as the pair chase fleeing villains through the streets of Los Angeles in their red Coyote.

The Coyote is actually a kit car based on the McLaren M6 GTR which was a sports racer. The kit was developed by Manta cars of California who reshaped the roof and took away the windows and the tops of the doors. I wonder why TV stars never seem to use doors in the way in which they were designed.

Though the original racers were V8 powered the Coyote, which is based on a modified VW Beetle floorpan, has 2.7-litre Porsche 911 power, and there is nothing wrong with that except for the sound which does not come across well on TV. Instead of a Porsche's distinctive sound, we have the noise of a dubbed-in CanAm V8. Oh, well, can't have everything.

McCormick, meanwhile, discovers that life on the right side of the law isn't so bad after all while Hardcastle sits in the passenger seat, in his Hawaiian shorts and loud shirts, loving every minute of it.

Magnum P.I.

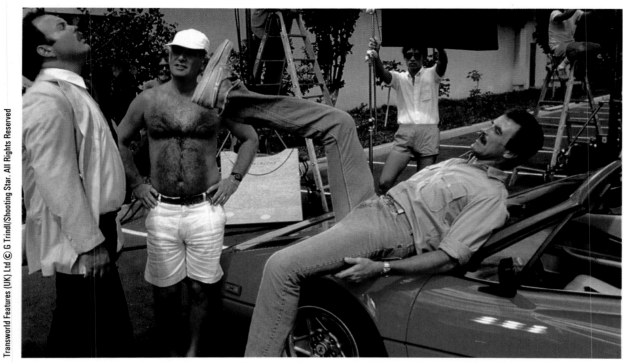

Magnum P.I., which started its successful TV screening in 1980, has made Tom Selleck a star. The TV plot follows the adventures of Thomas Magnum, an ex-Vietnam soldier who now works as a private eye. He has the good fortune to be awarded free accommodation at a wealthy writer's home in Hawaii, for whom he apparently once did a favour. That leaves all his earnings to go towards the insurance and maintenance of his rather beautiful Ferrari.

In this case, it is the Pininfarina-penned 308GTSi. Originally introduced as the 308GTB, Ferrari merely cut the middle out of the roof and called it the Spider, hence the S suffix. It is powered by a fuel-injected, 3-litre, transverse, mid-mounted, 90-degree V8 producing around 250 bhp and a top speed of more than 150 mph.

If there ever was a car which upset the enthusiasts, it was the fake Ferrari used in the TV series *Miami Vice*. They shouldn't really have got it wrong. Crockett and Tubbs are supposed to be street-wise cops using cars, boats and even money confiscated from drug dealers in order to establish enough cred' to infiltrate their world and arrest them. Then they can confiscate even more. If the crooks were in any way smarter than these two cops, then they would know right away that this is no Ferrari.

It may *look* like a 365GTS/4, commonly known as a Ferrari Daytona Spider, but under that cleverly-disguised fibreglass skin is a 1981 Chevrolet Corvette. The car is the creation of Tom McBurni's Coachcraft company in Santee, California. With real Spiders, which

were built between 1969 and 1974, fetching a quarter of a million dollars or more, driving them can be a reckless use of investment; there is therefore a ready market for replicas. But to anybody in the know, especially two smart cops, it is obviously not the real thing: the wheels are wrong, the windscreen is wrong and the noise is all wrong. Don't get me wrong—the sound, a rumbling purr, is fine for a Chevy V8 but the Ferrari had a screaming V12. This time the cops got taken for a ride.

They wise-up, though. In the latest series they get not one but two Ferraris, and this time they are real. The Testarossa is the latest in a long line of supercars from this Italian manufacturer. The controversial, but undeniably unique, design is the work of the Pininfarina studio and they also produce the body before it is

shipped to Maranello for assembly. There Ferrari add the important
ingredient: a four-valves per cylinder, flat-12 Boxer engine. With a
capacity a little under 5 litres, it produces 390 bhp and pushes the
Testarossa from 0–100 km/h in 5.8 seconds, with a top speed of
180.2 mph. Just what you need for catching criminals.

Filmed entirely on location on the French Riviera, *The Persuaders* provided ample opportunity for its two debonair crimefighters, Moore and Curtis, to drive some spectacular cars. These included a gold Aston Martin DB6, a 206GT Ferrari Dino, a Lancia Fulvia Spider and a Jensen Interceptor

Transworld Features (UK) Ltd

The Persuaders

Following the late 1960s, with such series as *Man In A Suitcase*, *The Avengers* and *The Man From U.N.C.L.E.*, the early 1970s arrived, and so, on British TV, did *The Persuaders*.

Roger Moore starred as Lord Brett Sinclair, a debonair British peer, and Tony Curtis starred as Danny Wilde, a Bronx-born millionaire. They became The Persuaders after a chance meeting in Nice, when a retired judge convinced them that a life of crime-busting would be beneficial for both of them. The series, which was filmed totally on the French Riviera, followed the exploits of these two 'handsome playboys'.

To assist them in keeping up with, and ultimately catching, the rotters, Sinclair drove the archetypel British sports car, an Aston Martin DB6, and Wilde drove a screaming red Ferrari Dino. On their worldwide travels, they also hopped in and out of Alfa Romeos, Lancias, and anything else that suited their image. The series was massively popular, although Moore had vowed not to appear in another television series after *The Saint*, which had finished two years previously, but I suppose he succumbed to persuasion.

The Adventurer

Gene Barry starred as The Adventurer, in the TV series of the same name. Although a majority of his time was spent jet-setting around in a chopper, when he came down to earth a stunning European sports car was always on hand, such as this early 1970s Maserati Ghibli

The Adventurer, originally produced for American television, was similar in vein to *The Persuaders* but, screened a year later in 1972, did not seem to capture the imagination. In fact, the scripts were so far-fetched, it seemed to saturate it more than anything.

Gene Barry played the role of Gene Brady, an international movie star who, in his spare time, was a top secret agent, working for a mysterious Mr Parmenter. The basic structure of the script dictated that almost week in, week out, Brady would be on the verge of commencing a shoot, when he would be called off the set to rescue a damsel, or dissident, in distress.

The Adventurer did not drive a 'set' car; in fact, he most frequently travelled in a helicopter, but, like The Persuaders, he always seemed to have a fast sports car at his disposal when out on an adventure.

7016RX06

Stingray

Photos courtesy of Stephen J Cannell Productions Inc.

The television series *Stingray* stars Nick Mancuso, who plays an undercover detective of that name, out, as usual, to rid the streets of the bad guys. He's the strong, silent type, who goes it alone when out on crime-busting missions. He does, however, have the company, appropriately enough, of a black 1965 Sting Ray. The Corvette features in a good deal of the programme, providing some exciting chase sequences. Although in its heyday the Sting Ray could only be caught by beasts like the Shelby Cobra, many modern cars give it (and therefore the viewers) a good run for its money.

General Motors offered two different engine sizes for their '65 model: a 327 cu. in., or the more powerful 396. Unfortunately for our illustrious detective, the huge 427 version was not available until a year later, in 1966. Almost all the '65s ran on four-speed manual transmission, and for the first time that year, four-wheel disc brakes were an optional extra.

Filming started on the series in 1985, and it has been a success ever since. The Vette is, of course, stunning and well worth seeing.

The Saint

In 1963, Roger Moore appeared on British television as Simon Templar, more commonly known as The Saint, a name that originated from Templar's habit of simply initialling his letters S.T. The series, an instant success, was based on the books by Leslie Charteris, and followed the hectic adventures of this dashing buccaneer, who was accompanied by a rather beautiful Volvo P1800E, with the number ST1.

In 1978, almost a decade after Roger Moore and his halo had disappeared from the small screen, *The Return Of The Saint* appeared. This was a rather weak sequel, seeming to just milk the original idea. It starred Ian Ogilvy as the new Saint, reintroduced using a rather feeble excuse about Templar's activities during the war. With a higher budget, Templar was now driving a white Jaguar XJS, but a problem had materialized relating to use of the ST1 number plate. There was a real car in England that possessed the registration ST1, and the owner simply refused to sell. This problem was apparently circumvented by simply filming almost all of the series abroad! Such difficulties no longer occur as police dispensation can be obtained to allow two or more cars to travel on the same plate in such special situations.

Of all the people I spoke to when compiling this book—and there were more than a few—stunt man, bike racer, director, driver and race car sponsor Hal Needham was perhaps the most enthusiastic. Despite his years in the industry he still made time to talk, and in our conversation was able to convey this enthusiasm for automobiles more than most.

Like Steve McQueen and James Garner, he has spent an awful lot of his leisure time racing around the deserts of California and Mexico, mostly on motorcycles, in events like the Baja and Mint 400. At work he is in the same business as McQueen and Garner but unlike them his face is hardly ever before the camera, because for 21 years Hal Needham has been the stunt man taking the risk, calculated maybe, but risk nevertheless.

The stunt man is usually the unsung hero but at one stage in his career Hal was approached by a toy company who wanted to produce a Hal Needham stunt doll. To promote it they needed something spectacular, something like Evel Knievel's canyon jump, around which they had also marketed a doll. Enter Bill Fredrick and the SMI-Motivator, a rocket car aimed at the sound barrier.

The toy company and Hal thought it would be just great if he could break the sound barrier—think of the publicity, think of the doll-ars. Well, Hal took the car out and ran an incredible 620 mph but during another run his breaking parachutes failed to open when he was going only 350 mph. Luckily, Hal survived the resultant crash but decided that 'a guy could get his ass busted' doing that. He still wanted to break the sound barrier but what he needed was 'some other dumb sombitch' to drive. Though by no means dumb, he found a driver in Stan Barrett and with a few dollars he made from directing *Smokey And The Bandit*, financed the Budweiser Rocket.

In the 1930s and 1940s they used to hold speed trials and hot rod races at Muroc Dry Lake in the Mojave Desert, but when the war came the US Air Force took over the area and established Edwards Air Force Base. In recent years it has been the home of the Space Shuttle but in 1979 it became the venue for Stan's incredible run of 739.666 mph. It may not be a speed recognized by the FIM because there was no back-up run, but when they looked at the wheel tracks and saw that the front wheel had been airborne, who in their right mind could consider going again? As far as Hal is concerned it's a record. I'm not going to argue.

Hal Needham's Speed of Sound, in the hands of Stan Barrett, surpassing Mach I on 17 December 1979. The recorded speed was 739.666 mph

Right Racing the roads across America demands some sort of Q car. Hal and Brock Yates chose this ambulance for the real 1978 transcontinent Cannonball race (on which the film was based) between Connecticut and the Portofino Inn in Redondo Beach, California

The Bandits from left to right: driver Harry Gant, Burt Reynolds, crew chief Travis Carter and owner Hal Needham

His career as a director began with the release of *Smokey And The Bandit* in 1977. As you would expect, it's one long stunt starring Burt Reynolds as the bootlegger and Jackie Gleason as the cop, and it is good. This was followed by another same-team effort in 1980 with the obvious title *Smokey And The Bandit II*. Though not as good as the original, it was far better than number three which followed but was not directed by Hal. He, meanwhile, had been directing Burt in the 1978 release *Hooper*. This was a comical and quite good look at an ageing stunt man being pressurized to make the big jump by his young protégé, played by Jan-Michael Vincent. Finally, well, so far, there was *The Cannonball Run* and its sequel. Though booed by the critics, they were good, fun car films, featured on pages 78–81.

Away from the set, Hal for the past half-dozen years have been both participating in and sponsoring NASCAR racing. He competes in the Sportsman class but his Skoal Bandit Chevy (number 33) is driven by Harry Gant and competes in the Grand National series. Though

the rules say these must be standard-shaped American sedans with a maximum of 358 cu. in. and just one carburettor, they still produce over 600 bhp and can exceed 200 mph. Not a car for the road, you might think. Wrong!

Recently Hal and Harry decided to enter the car in a 125-mile Mexican road race called La Carrera between San Felipe and Ensenada. They won, covering the distance in just 54.14 minutes, but had a few hairy moments overtaking truck-loads of Mexicans who had not had the message that the road was closed for a race. Could this, like the Cannonball Run, be the plot for a film? Watch out, at a cinema near you . . . .

Moon buggys are not available second-hand, so when a film or TV company want a special vehicle they call upon a hard-working, dedicated band of customizers for whom no idea is too ridiculous, no project too difficult and no deadline impossible

Finally, a look into the heart of it all; an insight into the men who make it all happen— the guys that build the cars. They should not be dismissed as workshop labourers who beat the odd irregular showbiz panel— almost all of their commissioned work requires their own design, and if it doesn't, it's because the studios have probably only given them about five minutes to build the car.

For many years the word 'customizer' or 'hot rodder' has not conjured up the most respected of impressions. All I ask is for you to read about the people in this chapter, and make up your own mind.

Imagine the lives they have carved out for themselves, and you may feel a twinge of envy; but whether you do or not, take a close look at the cars featured in this book, and try and imagine, in your wildest dreams, that you could have come up with such beautiful designs and original ideas; and if you reckon that it wouldn't have been a problem, then at least have the decency to admit that there is no way on earth you could have built them.

There is a saying: 'A Devil with a hammer, and Hell with a torch'. Nothing could be more true.

George Barris

When George Barris started messing around with balsa wood back in 1932, at the age of seven, I doubt if anyone could have imagined that 50 years on he would be held in high regard as one of the most inspired and imaginative auto-stylists, known simply as King of the Kustomizers. However, he cannot merely be categorized as a talented customizer—his work on experimental vehicles for Ford, General Motors and Chrysler will prove that.

By the age of 13, Barris had already customized his first car, a 1925 Buick. With a few more radically styled creations under his belt, it was time to move to Los Angeles, home of the hot rod and centre of the customizing world. George and his brother Sam set up shop in Lynwood, California, in 1945. They merrily chopped tops, frenched headlights and, while doing so, created a style that would later become popularly known as the lead sled.

It was the late 1940s, and Barris, realizing the importance of publicity, was photographing and writing short articles about his creations. As these began to appear in the various auto-enthusiast magazines, public interest spread. Soon he was getting commissions from various events organizers to create 'crowd pulling' cars. This led to interest from the movie industry and, ultimately, a job in Hollywood as the industry's technical adviser.

That was in 1950, and since then, Barris has produced many cars; his client list is, to say the least, impressive. Ferraris for Clint Eastwood, Lincolns for Jayne Mansfield and Tony Curtis, Cadillacs for Dean Martin and Elvis Presley, and so it goes on. But what Barris is probably most famous for is his work with the television companies: the Beverly Hillbillies' 1921 Oldsmobile truck and 1925 Oldsmobile hot rod; the Adams Family Packard Phaeton, and the extremely popular Munsters Coach.

Barris was given three days to come up with an idea for a suitable Munster-mobile, and the Coach was born. Based on a 1923 Model T body, the Coach was powered by a Ford Cobra engine, with Jahns high-dome pistons and an Isky cam, and it inhaled through ten chrome carbs. The body was painted with 40 coats of hand-rubbed black pearl, and almost all the peripheral items were finished in gold-leaf. That included the 'gravestone' radiator, casket door handles, and gas-lantern headlights with their spider-web glass. The interior was red velvet with ermine rugs on the floor!

The Munsters also owned Drag-U-La, which was a dragster based around a real coffin that Barris had lengthened by 3 ft. Grandpa used the Drag-U-La in a race against Hermann in the Coach, and in true dragster style, Grandpa was positioned behind the 351 Ford Mustang engine. The radiator was a miniature casket made in solid brass, the grille a marble gravestone, and the hub caps were decorated with solid silver spiders. Chrome organ exhaust pipes completed the effect.

However, surely Barris' most famous creation to date, which went on to become a comic-book cult and, ultimately, the most famous custom car ever created, was the Batmobile.

The origins of the Batmobile, built in the mid-1960s, go back to New York's Central Park, and the unusual launch of an extremely unusual car. The year was 1955, and Ford, in conjunction with the Ghia design studios in Turin, had created what they liked to call a 'dream car'. The Lincoln Futura looked, to say the least, like a figment of someone's

imagination, and it certainly demanded a sensational launch—a showroom presentation just would not have been appropriate. Hence the Lincoln Futura, that most fabulously-finned Ford, made its first public appearance in Central Park, creating a sensation.

Back to the mid-1960s and Kustom City, the workshops of George Barris. ABC Television, who made the TV series, gave Barris three weeks to build the car. Having decided on the Futura as a base—it already had a twin-bubble cockpit, deeply hooded headlights and massive

rear fins—Barris started work. First of all, he lengthened the chassis to 21 ft, then a Thunderbird 428 cu. in. V8 engine was dropped into place. The whole of the body underwent a fibreglass re-styling—the front end was designed to resemble the face of a bat, with the grille, or 'mouth', concealing a set of rockets. Other special devices were a set of parachutes for quick braking (and they worked!); a Batscope, which consisted of a revolving closed-circuit camera supplying Batman with 360-degree vision; and a Bateye anti-theft device. The Batmobile was finished with 40 layers of black-velvet bat fuzz. Five separate Batmobiles were produced altogether to satisfy show demand, the original costing $75,000, with the other four, as moulds off the original, being a mere $40,000 apiece!

From its first appearance on the ABC TV series, the Batmobile was an astounding success, attracting massive public interest. As with most of Barris' creations, they were reproduced as scale models by companies such as Revell and AMT. The mini-Batmobiles sold in their thousands; the public desire was, and still is, insatiable.

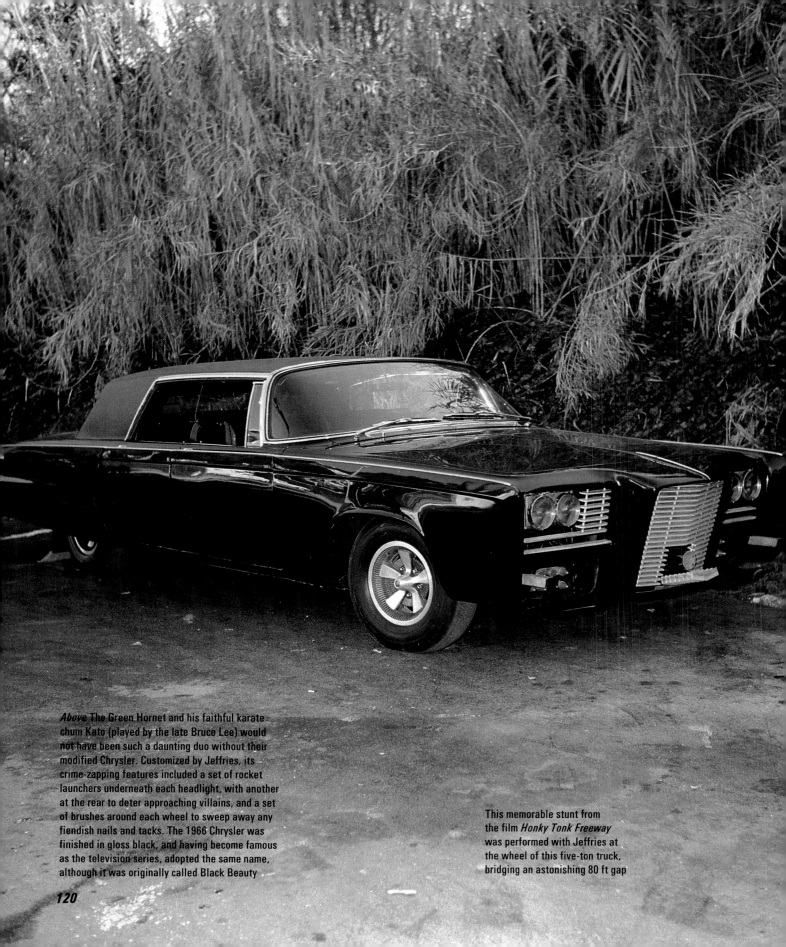

Above The Green Hornet and his faithful karate chum Kato (played by the late Bruce Lee) would not have been such a daunting duo without their modified Chrysler. Customized by Jeffries, its crime-zapping features included a set of rocket launchers underneath each headlight, with another at the rear to deter approaching villains, and a set of brushes around each wheel to sweep away any fiendish nails and tacks. The 1966 Chrysler was finished in gloss black, and having become famous as the television series, adopted the same name, although it was originally called Black Beauty

This memorable stunt from the film *Honky Tonk Freeway* was performed with Jeffries at the wheel of this five-ton truck, bridging an astonishing 80 ft gap

Dean Jeffries

Dean Jeffries, renowned for his skills as a movie car builder, paint expert and stunt man, was born in the right town—Compton, in California, is somewhere very close to the heart of the hot rod world. While Jeffries was still in high school, experimenting with different finishes on his '32 Chevy coupé, Compton was already the home of two rodding legends.

Ed 'Big Daddy' Roth was bringing imagination into the third dimension with his stunning show cars, such as the Beatnik Bandit and the Outlaw; and Von Dutch, father of the pin-stripe, was adding his own special finishing touches to an endless flow of cars.

It followed that after Jeffries had picked up a few hints from his neighbours, he would open up his own shop, which he did, on Atlantic Boulevard. His business, which specialized in painting and striping, was a success, but having built up a solid reputation, Jeffries found himself wanting more demanding work.

The early 1960s saw him searching for new challenges at the Indianapolis 500. He became an annual visitor as the drivers' demands for his elaborate paintwork increased. It was a busy time for Jeffries, but while working at the trackside he was picking up new skills from the drivers and mechanics, so he enjoyed this stimulating period.

The techniques that he had learnt at the Indy 500 were to prove invaluable a few years later when he was invited to enter the prestigious Oakland Roadster Show. Utilizing these new skills in frame fabrication and sheet-metal work, he was able to construct a stunning asymmetrical single-seater hot rod, which he called the Manta Ray. Based on a pre-war Grand Prix Maserati frame, the Manta Ray looked wild with its vacuum-formed acrylic bubble top; this canopy and the ignition could both be operated by remote control. It was powered by a Ford 289 engine, and originally possessed down-draught Weber carbs.

Dean Jeffries and his Manta Ray left the 1964 Oakland Roadster Show with the 10 ft high gold trophy, the most coveted prize in the hot-rodding world. As a sign of how much that trophy meant to Jeffries, it is interesting to note that he still owns the Manta Ray and awards it pride of place in his showroom.

The mid-1960s saw Jeffries in his heyday for, a year after winning Oakland, he was commissioned to build his first major showbiz car: the Monkeemobile. To this day, it is one of Jeffries' most famous and popular creations. Based on a 1966 Pontiac GTO, he lengthened the front end, whipped the roof off, and removed the trunk. He then added a Phaeton-style hood, and finished it in candy-red paint. The Monkeemobile also came with a trailer that would unfold to form an impromptu stage. In the same year, Jeffries built his other most famous car, Black Beauty, a modified '66 Chrysler Imperial that was used in the children's television series *The Green Hornet*. Both were resounding successes, highlighted by their scale-model versions selling by the thousand. The Monkeemobile and Black Beauty also firmly cemented Jeffries' relationship with the world of the stars.

He went on to build the *Diamonds Are Forever* Moon Buggy—his first science-fiction creation; the Landmaster from *Damnation Alley*;

and all the weird cars used in *Death Race 2000* and *Logan's Run*.

Jeffries is also an extremely talented stunt man. He has nearly 50 films to his credit, for both building the cars and doing the stunt work. One of his most memorable stunts took place in *Honky Tonk Freeway*, in which he co-ordinated and performed what must be one of the most complex stunts in cinema history. It involved 23 cars, a truck full of oranges, a blown-up bridge, and Jeffries behind the wheel of a five-ton truck. The stunt culminates with Jeffries jumping the truck across the 80 ft gap in the bridge.

If you are wondering what an extraordinary man like Dean Jeffries does in his spare time, well, he doesn't have very much. But he does own the only Ford GT40 roadster in the world, so when there's a quiet moment . . . .

We put it all together.
The AnyCar Loan.

'29 Hudson
'71 Continental
'71 Mach I
'66 Corvette
'61 Valiant
'68 Ford
'67 Volkswagen
'73 Plymouth
'69 Toronado
'54 Chrysler
Dodge
'69 Cadillac
'73 Triumph
'73 Toyota
'58 Volvo
'70 Pontiac
'61 Imperial
'70 Mustang
Catalina
'73 Mercedes

Get any car—new, used, sporty or sensible—with 180 days to shop around for the best deal.

Unlike many of his contemporaries, and the thousands of cars that have passed through his hands, Gene Winfield keeps a low profile; he doesn't even have a sign outside his shop. But, just like many of his contemporaries, he has been messing around with cars ever since his days in high school.

Fresh from graduation, Winfield set up a paint and panel shop in partnership with his two brothers, and by 1947 he had his own little business, Windy's Custom Shop. He has been working on cars for over 40 years—when I said he had worked on *thousands* of cars, it was no exaggeration. Also, he has probably performed a more varied range of auto work than any of the legendary figures he is affiliated with.

He has painted, panelled, chopped and channelled just like everybody else. But he has also worked for scale-model companies, advertising agencies and, of course, the television and movie industries. One of his most beautiful screen creations is *The Man From U.N.C.L.E.* sports car; then there is the *Bonnie And Clyde* car; plus a various assortment that appeared in *Blade Runner*, *Magnum Force*, *Star Trek*, and a remarkable convertible Camaro that appeared on the *Dean Martin Show*. What made the Camaro so special was its ability to change into a '31 Chevy roadster, something a troop of 30 dancers proved on the show.

The Dean Martin car(s) was a typical Winfield creation. He rarely builds totally improbable show-type cars, but the alterations he performs on everyday production cars have to be seen to be believed.

The Any Car, built for Hanover Insurance to demonstrate their willingness to insure almost anything, is a case in point. It was based on a Pontiac, and was 'compiled' from over 30 different cars; the result was monstrous, but, in its own ugly way, a work of art. Then there is the Chevy, or rather half of it, that Chevrolet commissioned for a commercial; he simply had to cut the car in half, straight down the middle, and make sure it was still perfectly driveable! As if that was not enough, he also worked for a time with AMT, one of the biggest scale-model manufacturers. Winfield was employed to reverse the whole process, building life-size versions of the AMT models.

His main interest, however, lies in the late-1940s and early-1950s cars, especially the fat-fendered Fords. Realizing how rare and sought-after these were becoming, Winfield produced a fibreglass replica body. So, if you happen to want a late-1940s lead sled, but cannot find one, Winfield's your man.

Gene Winfield is, quite simply, capable of anything. You want it built, he'll build it. Were it not for his personal project Model T roadster that he has so far been building since 1958, and the car he built for *Mission Impossible*, I don't think he'd know those words existed.

Gene Winfield

Far left One of Winfield's weird and wonderful creations ready to roll. This futuristic machine was built for the TV series *Logan's Run*

Left A true publicity machine : the Any Car, commissioned by Hanover Insurance to demonstrate that they would, literally, insure 'any car'. Winfield utilized parts from over 30 different models to create this hideous beast

The Man from U.N.C.L.E. car, star of the TV series of the same name, was definitely one of Winfield's most beautiful creations. It is pictured here with the stars displaying the gull-wing doors, and a brunette displaying something else !

Eddie Paul has been working on cars at his shop, Customs by Eddie, for about 15 years now, which makes him one of the new breed of celebrity car customizers. He started out, like so many of his contemporaries, messing about with his own car while still at high school. The car was a 1950 Chevy, and it must have been pretty impressive, because before long he was working on his classmates' cars.

His big break came in 1977 with a telephone call from Paramount Studios. They were in trouble, having commissioned some cars to be built by a guy who simply hadn't produced the goods; could he do the work? Yes—which is the standard answer if a film company would like you to build some cars, but this was not the standard request.

Most movie work requires a special car, maybe even two, and they often need it finished within a few weeks; Paramount, on the other hand, didn't just want the odd car, they wanted 30! They also wanted them completed in 14 days! Needless to say, Eddie, with the help of some extremely hard workers, did it. The film was Grease, and the cars were superb—you can read more about the

T-Birds' Greased Lightnin', White Lightnin' and the Scorpions' Hell's Chariot in a separate *Grease* feature on pages 84–85.

When you can do work like that, within such short notice, the Hollywood grapevine swings into action, and soon everybody's desperate for your help. Eddie reckons that most studios know a long time in advance what cars they will need, but just don't bother getting organized until the last minute—what's the point when people like Eddie can almost guarantee they will get it done, even if that means tomorrow.

Eddie has also built the original General Lee for *The Dukes Of Hazzard*, and was involved in the pre-01 days, as well as cars for *Cobra* (see pages 56–57, *Streets Of Fire*, and *Innerspace*, the new Steven Spielberg production. He is also, like fellow craftsman Dean Jeffries, a talented stunt driver. His credits include *Gone In 60 Seconds*, *The Mask*, *Junkman*, *Streets Of Fire*, and some of those amazing Hazzard leaps.

It is good to see a new face emulate heights that I was beginning to think customizers could only reach if they had started work in the 1940s. Congratulations, Mr Paul.

Above This graphic Trans Am was customized by Eddie, for use in the film *The Junk Man*

Left Two of Eddie Paul's personal '66 Mustangs, which were built as project cars for *Hot Rod* magazine

Right A break in filming of an early *Dukes Of Hazzard* episode, which featured a race between the General Lee and an unsuccessful Camaro. Eddie located, bought and built the Camaro, along with its twin understudy, within three days!

Writing a book is a long, hair-tearing process. *Star Cars* has been no different, except that it was done in record time and involved a lot more barbering than usual because of the difficulty in reaching the right people and finding the right pictures. There are, therefore, an awful lot of people to thank who, one way or another, made the journey possible. Besides everybody who is in the book, I would like to thank the following:

Aston Martin
Autocar magazine
Auto Image
B H Associates
Jeff Bloxham
CC magazine
Mike Collins
Columbia Pictures
Goldcrest Films & TV Ltd
Golden Communications
HB Halicki Productions
Hot VWs magazine
ITC Entertainment Ltd
James Dean Foundation
London Features International
David Long
Lotus Cars Ltd
Motor magazine
MPL Communications
New Century Productions
Nissan Motor Corporation
Nitro magazine
Paramount Picture Corporation
Paramount Television Ltd
Promotional Displays Inc.
Renault UK Ltd
Rex Features Ltd
Eric Sawyer
Stephen J Cannell Productions
The Sunday Times colour magazine
Transworld Features Syndicate
Hans-Jürgen Tücherer
Twentieth-Century-Fox Film Corporation
United Artists Pictures Inc.
VW Trends magazine
Walt Disney Productions
Warner Brothers Inc.

Finally, I would especially like to thank my family for providing all the cups of tea and putting up with my tantrums, and Tony, for lending me the word processor, and whose whole idea it was.